Robert Knightley

Alfrede or Right Reinthron'd

A Translation of William Drury's

Aluredus sive Alfredus

MEDIEVAL & RENAISSANCE TEXTS & STUDIES

VOLUME 99

Robert Knightley

Alfrede or Right Reinthron'd

A Translation of William Drury's

Aluredus sive Alfredus

EDITED BY

Albert H. Tricomi

Medieval & Renaissance texts & studies
Binghamton, New York
1993

Library of Congress Cataloging-in-Publication Data

Drury, William, d. ca. 1641.
[Aluredus sive Alfredus. English]
Alfrede, or, Right reinthron'd / by Robert Knightley ; a translation of William Drury's Aluredus sive Alfredus ; edited by Albert H. Tricomi.
p. cm. — (Medieval & Renaissance texts & studies ; v. 99)
A new old-spelling edition with notes and commentary of a translation by Knightley ca. 1659 of Drury's 1619 work.
Includes bibliographical references.
ISBN 0-86698-113-6
1. Alfred, King of England, 849–899—Drama. 2. Great Britain—History—Alfred, 871–899—Drama. 3. College and school drama, Latin (Medieval and modern)—France—Douai—Translations into English. I. Knightley, Robert. II. Tricomi, Albert H., 1942- III. Title. IV. Title: Alfrede. V. Title: Right reinthron'd.
PA8485.D75A813 1992
872'.04—dc20 92-31804
CIP

∞

This book is made to last.
It is set in Palatino, smythe-sewn
and printed on acid-free paper
to library specifications

Printed in the United States of America

Table of Contents

Acknowledgments

Research for this edition has been generously supported by a 1990 Experienced Faculty Travel Award from the United University Professions, and by separate grants, in 1987 and 1989, from the American Philosophical Society and the Graduate School of SUNY Binghamton. The assistance of these organizations permitted me to launch the project and to bring it to conclusion.

The edition would not have attained its present, more comprehensive form were it not for Lois Potter. She pointed out to me the remarkable fact (first noted by her in 1981 in *The Revels History of Drama in English* 4:267) that Knightley's *Alfrede or Right Reinthron'd* is a translation of William Drury's Latin play *Aluredus sive Alfredus*. The interconnectedness of these works, especially with respect to the production of Catholic high culture in the seventeenth century, proceeds from her fundamental insight. I am pleased to acknowledge my gratitude publicly.

All of the publisher's readers provided scrupulous readings of the transcription and made wise editorial suggestions. I received superb technical assistance from the staff of the Bodleian library, and particularly from Dr. Bruce Charles Barker-Benfield, who assisted me in examining the physical characteristics and quiring of Bodleian MS. Rawlinson. poet. 80. The editorial staff of MRTS, especially Judith Sumner, Michael Pavese, Katharine S. Mascaro and Catherine R. Di Cesare, provided steadfast assistance and support, as has the director of MRTS, Mario Di Cesare.

I am also pleased to record debts of gratitude to my colleagues in Renaissance literature, Alvin Vos and Norman Burns, who discussed the conception and execution of this project with me at various stages of its development, and to Zoja Pavlovskis, my colleague in comparative literature, who reviewed my Latin citations and provided an English translation of Drury's Epilogue to *Aluredus*. My wife Bet, and Al, Will, and Eebie were, as usual, always part of this project, both in work and in play.

Introduction

The translation of William Drury's *Aluredus sive Alfredus* (1619) by one who identified himself merely as "R. K." amounts to a good deal more than just the Englishing of a Latin play. Drury was an English priest and well-known academic dramatist at the English College at Douai. He also spent many years on the English mission as a confessor and several times suffered imprisonment in the course of carrying out his duties. His *Aluredus*, a quasi-historical play eulogizing Alfred's Christian virtue following the king's defeat by the Danes in 878 and his subsequent reinstatement, was composed to instruct and fortify in the faith the English students at Douai.

The circumstances surrounding the translation of *Aluredus* on the eve of the Restoration under the new title *Alfrede or Right Reinthron'd* attest to the play's political function of heralding analogically the re-enthronement of the Stuarts in the person of Charles II. Featuring St. Cuthbert as Alfrede's patron saint, *Alfrede* is also one of the rare plays in seventeenth-century England to depict a Catholic saint and to give voice to the ideals of an outlawed religion. Even more significant is the fact that the translator, who belonged to a prominent Catholic family, dedicated *Alfrede* to Lady (Mary) Blount, who herself had been born into a distinguished Catholic family and had married into another. An examination of the network of interconnections among these gentry families provides an unusual, important demonstration of how the making and transmission of high culture fostered Anglo-Catholic ideals. In the face of a half-century of oppression and darkening prospects, *Aluredus* and its English reincarnation, *Alfrede*, functioned to sustain what had clearly become a minority faith.

The Manuscript

The sole text of *Alfrede or Right Reinthron'd* (1659) is Bodleian MS. Rawlinson. poet. 80. Richard Rawlinson (1689/90–1755), a graduate of Oxford and a great book collector, donated the manuscript to his university along with the rest of the considerable collection that bears his name. *Alfrede* appears in a small bound volume whose pages are 18.7 centimeters in length, 13.6 centimeters in width.[1] The paper is sturdy

---

[1] The Bodleian Library's *A Summary Catalogue of Western Manuscripts in the Bodleian Library at Oxford*, ed. Falconer Madan (Oxford: Clarendon Press, 1953)

and thick so that the usual problems of leeching are virtually nonexistent. The leather binding, however, is brittle, cracked, and warped. Along the outer edge, written in an eighteenth-century hand, are the faded vestiges of the play's title, "Alfrede [ ] Trag. Com[.] R. K. MS."

The manuscript was bound in the eighteenth century while in Rawlinson's possession and displays on the inside board cover a Rawlinson bookplate of a sitting scholar, inscribed with the words "Sigillum Univ. Oxon."[2] The introduction of thirteen blank leaves preceding the manuscript proper and eleven more (unnumbered) at the end dates from this period. The original manuscript is 62 leaves numbered in pencil, inclusive of the dedication and epilogue; hence the Bodleian description of the manuscript as xiii + 73 leaves.[3]

---

records the manuscript's length as 7⅝" (3:298). This figure corresponds to the size of the cover rather than the paper.

[2] For a reproduction and discussion of Rawlinson's bookplates see B. J. Enright, "Richard Rawlinson, Collector, Antiquary, and Topographer" (Doctoral diss., Oxford University, 1959), ante 106.

[3] *Summary Catalogue*, 298. For the following, more technical description of the manuscript, I am indebted to Dr. Bruce Charles Barker-Benfield, Bodleian Librarian. The general description I have provided concerning the construction of the *Alfrede* volume is corroborated by an analysis of the quiring and by beta-radiology reproductions of the watermarks. The pages that precede the manuscript proper comprise a single gathering of fourteen leaves, the first of which has been pasted into the inside board cover (and is therefore not counted as one of the thirteen blank leaves). Sheets have been bifoliated and cut to produce four leaves. Leaves are paired as follows: board page–xiii, i–xii, ii–xi, iii–x, iv–ix, etc. Leaf iv is a two-inch stub bearing the horizontal chain lines characteristic of the other leaves. Leaf xiii, which precedes the manuscript proper, is marbled and, distinctively, bears vertical chain lines. Unnumbered leaves 63–73 are similarly quired so that the first leaf is paired with the last, and so on. Leaf 63 is also marbled and, along with 64, was either snipped or worked into the outer board and pasted down. Such pasting down is evident with folio 65, whose second half has become the inside facing of the end board. Subsequent sheets are foliated so that 66 matches with 73, 67 with 72, 68 with 71, and 69 with 70. The watermarks appearing on both of these later quirings are comprised of a coat of arms with elaborate crown accompanied by the initials "G. R." for George Rex, an insignia that places the date of binding between 1714, when the first George ascended the English throne, and 1755, the year of Rawlinson's death.

The two watermarks on the original leaves of the *Alfrede* manuscript are quite different, as is the quiring. The first is a fleur-de-lis with wreathed insignia "I G A" at the bottom. The figure of such a fleur-de-lis with shield or wreath is similar to a 1662 watermark recorded in W. A. Churchill's *Watermarks in Paper in England, France, etc. in the XVIIIII and XVIII Centuries and their Interconnections* [(Amsterdam: Menns Hertzberge & Co., 1935), plate 631] and is almost a century earlier than the watermarks on the blank leaves of the bound manuscript.

Foliation accounts for this watermark's appearing on half the leaves from 1–35 (the others bear no watermark). Similarly, on half the leaves from 36–62 there appears a rose with unelaborated crown. The foliation has resulted in the fleurs-de-lis appearing on different pages from those that bear the insignia; the same is true of the rose with crown. This separation becomes an aid in determining the

Written in fair copy in a single, brisk hand, the manuscript is almost surely scribal and appears to have been made from an authorial exemplar. There are no major substantive alterations in the manuscript—six cancellations of single words and two cancelled stage directions. Although apostrophes are sometimes carelessly placed, the effort to present a tidied transcription is apparent in the numerous careted insertions of a letter or two. Other interpolations are limited to single words, neatly interlineated. There are many false starts, particularly in the writing of certain syllables before the necessary preceding syllables have been recorded.

In addition to scribal interpolations, corrections were made by superimposition. The original (suppressed) letters, where still visible, often look washed out in comparison to the rest of the text, suggesting that the scribe resorted to blotting to minimize the effects of his errors. More uncertain is the possibility that the scribe occasionally corrected the manuscript by scraping the original ink with a knife point. In several places the manuscript is abraded in places where corrections have been introduced.

A tendency toward crowding is observable at the bottoms of pages, especially from 20 to 24 and from page 50 on, where the letters are smaller and there is less space between lines. The signs of flagging efficiency are more apparent in these sections. In addition to an increase in the number of superimposed letters, catchwords, which appear appropriately throughout the manuscript, are missing three times consecutively from 20v to 21v and again at 24v and 25. From these inconclusive data, we may surmise that the manuscript was transcribed in two or possibly three sittings.

The likelihood that the play was transcribed from an exemplar may be observed in the following examples: "Pardon my loue if I haue iniured / y^{r} Name, by a fraudulent but pious / Calumniation" (1.14.58–60). The "y^{r}" has been superimposed over the still legible words "by a." But "by a" occurs later in the line, suggesting that the scribe, in attempting to make fair copy from another manuscript, jumped ahead (mind before hand), composing "by a" before writing "y^{r} Name." Similarly, in the phrase "y^{e}/ sporting armes of the soft embracing winds" (2.1.5–6), a washed out "of" precedes the "a" in "armes" and is a good example of what appears to be scribal metathesis. In the behest "Put that Care out of y^{r} Mind" (2.8.43), the "o" in "out" was originally written "of" as if the copyist were anticipating the next word.

---

quiring. Unlike the blank outer leaves, these are quired simply in units of four (leaves 1–4; 5–8; 9–12, etc.). This quiring is regular except that a stub, which would match leaf 17, appears between leaves 19 and 20. Also, leaf 62 is uncut at the top, giving us a 62A and 62B. These leaves match those marked 60 and 61.

Evidence for the scribe's being the author himself is weak. There are no interpolations as long as a single verse or prose line, or even a partial line of verse. The one kind of substantive correction that does occur appears in just two instances, where stage directions have been obliterated. In the first, an obliteration almost 2 centimeters long followed by another beneath it of 2.5 centimeters appears near the margin at the end of Act 4, scene 6. The second, occurring after the marginal direction "*Stru: peepes out*" (2.6.1), shows the attempted obliteration with innumerable curling overstrokes across the entire second part of the direction (approximately 2 x 2.5 centimeters). It is worth examining each of these closely.

The attempted obliteration of the second-act stage direction can be discerned almost in its entirety. The cancelled words appear to be "*Stru gets into / ye body of . . . / of ye tree and peeps out of / ye top.*" This direction, occurring at the beginning of the scene, is, however, partially restored at line 13, with the direction Strumbo "*gets into / the tree,*" and the remainder is restored at line 57 with the direction "*peeps out of the tree.*" The change is thus not substantive; it rearranges what is already present. The reason for this tinkering appears to be that the original direction was placed too early, since lines 9–11 show Strumbo observing, "the / Body of that tree w^ch^ . . . is hollow" and resolving to "enter into it." The alteration is then a matter of making the stage direction conform to the requirements of the text, not of deleting a substantive direction.

The other obliterated stage direction, 2–2.5 centimeters in length, is of a similar sort. The hypothesis that this change too, can be explained as an error cancellation provides the means for determining its content. In the manuscript, scenes 6 and 7 of Act 4 are of almost equal length, 29 and 30 lines respectively. This seventh scene, like the sixth, bears a two-line (uncancelled) stage direction at the end of the scene: "*exeunt / all but str: Cra:.*" Each line of this direction is the same in length as the corresponding line of the cancelled one. Using it as an exemplar, the obliterated stage direction can be read; it proves to be identical to that which appears in the next scene. As the scribe was completing 2.6., his eye evidently fell on the subsequent scene (of like length) with the result that the concluding stage direction for scene 7 was written prematurely. Realizing the error, the scribe obliterated the direction in 2.6.

Since even these alterations, the most substantive in the manuscript, introduce no original material, they provide strong reason to conclude that the entire transcription of *Alfrede* is scribal.

The Author, William Drury

The Drurys were a noted gentry family whose two main branches can be traced back to the beginning of the Tudor dynasty.[4] Sir Robert Drury, Henry VII's Speaker of the House and a privy councillor, bequeathed his estate to his first and second sons, Sirs William and Robert, respectively, from whom the two main branches devolved. Neither branch accepted Henry VIII's creation of an English church independent of Rome. From Sir William's side descended, in the late Elizabethan period, the recusant Henry Drury (d. 1586), his namesake son, who became a Jesuit lay brother, and the famous Catholic friend of John Donne, Sir Robert Drury (1575–1616), for whose deceased child, Elizabeth, the poet composed the "Anniversaries."[5]

From the second main branch descended the dramatist William Drury (1584–1641?), the third of six children whose father, also named William (d. 1589), was the famous judge of the prerogative court and whose mother, Mary (Southwell), was a kinswoman of the Jesuit poet Robert Southwell. William's father converted to Catholicism on his death bed, and William himself reported being received into the Catholic church by Father Henry Standish in 1601 at the suggestion of his eldest sister, Bridget.[6]

After commencing his schooling in London, he completed his

---

[4] The principal sources for William Drury's family history are *The Responsa Scholarum of the English College, Rome,* Part 1, 1598–1621, ed. Anthony Kenny (London: Catholic Record Society, 1962), 54: 151–53); Arthur Freeman, "William Drury, Dramatist," *Recusant History,* ed. A. F. Allison and D. M. Rogers, Catholic Record Society, 8 (1966): 293–97; Godfrey Anstruther, *The Seminary Priests, A Dictionary of the Secular Clergy of England and Wales 1558–1850* (Great Wakering, Essex: Mayhew-McCrimmon, 1975), 2:87–89; Henry Foley, *Records of the English Province of the Society of Jesus,* 7 vols. (London, 1875–83; repr. New York: Johnson Repr. Corporation, 1966); and *Douay College Diaries, Third, Fourth and Fifth, 1598–1654,* ed. Edwin H. Burton and Thomas L. Williams (London: Catholic Record Society, 1911). Although dated, Edgar Hall's account of Drury's life is his University of Chicago Ph.D. thesis, "William Drury's *Alvredus sive Alfredus*" (1918), 1–9, is useful. Michael Siconolfi's 1982 Syracuse University Ph.D. Thesis, "Robert Squire's *Death, A Comedie,*" offers the fullest modern reconstruction of the life (9–57), and I generally follow his method of presentation. The treatments of Drury's life and family relations in G. E. Bentley's *The Jacobean and Caroline Stage,* 7 vols. (Oxford: Clarendon Press, 1941–68), 3:290–91; *The Dictionary of National Biography,* 22 vols. (Oxford: Oxford Univ. Press, 1906), s.v. "Drury."; and Joseph Gillow's *A Literary and Biographical History or Bibliographical Dictionary of the English Catholics from the Breach with Rome to the Present Time* (London, 1885–1902), 2:110, are fragmentary and sometimes misleading.

[5] For a full account of the Drurys as a Catholic family in relation to Donne's own, see Robert C. Bald, *Donne and the Drurys* (Cambridge: Cambridge Univ. Press, 1959).

[6] Foley 1:77n.

studies in the humanities at St. Omer's in France. On 9 October 1605, along with his younger brother, Robert, who was later to become a Jesuit priest famous for his part in the "Fatal Vespers" of 1623, he enrolled at the English College at Rome under the family alias (used by Catholic gentry families for safety's sake) of Bedford.[7] William provided all this information to the admissions officers at the College at Rome, where he received minor orders in 1606.[8] In April 1610 he was ordained; two years later to the month he was sent on the English mission.[9]

Sometime while carrying out his missionary work, Drury was arrested and imprisoned in the Gatehouse. He was released and exiled on 26 June 1618, along with twenty-five other recusants in London prisons, at the order of James I, as a gesture of reconciliation to the departing, long-time Spanish ambassador to England, Count Gondomar.[10] The count sailed for the Continent on 15 July, evidently taking with him the priests and seminarians who had been released to him.[11] Filled with gratitude for the part Count Gondomar had played in securing his freedom and, presumably, for his help in obtaining a position at Douai (see below), Drury dedicated the 1620 edition of *Aluredus* to the former Spanish ambassador.

Following a meeting in Brussels in September 1618 between Gondomar and Matthew Kellison, president of the English College at Douai, the exiled Drury, who had remained under Gondomar's protection, returned with Kellison and was appointed to teach music to the younger students in Douai's humanities program. By 8 October, following an outbreak of the plague, Drury, along with another professor, was placed in charge of all the students in rhetoric and poetry at the College.[12] After settling in, Drury began to compose the Latin plays on which his reputation rests. On 8 January 1619 the students performed in the refectory, "privatim," an unnamed comedy by Drury—perhaps *Aluredus,* perhaps *Mors*—that was so well received that it was shown publicly three days later.[13] This record of the play's surprising success may explain why regular presentations of plays begin to appear in the *Douay Diaries* subsequent to this date. The tragicomedy *Aluredus* and the comedy *Mors* appeared in print in 1620.

---

[7] Foley 1:77n.

[8] *Responsa Scholarum* 151–53.

[9] Freeman, 294, 296n.

[10] *Acts of the Privy Council, 1617–19,* n.s., ed. John R. Dasent (London, 1890), 197–98.

[11] *Acts, Privy Council* 197–98.

[12] *Douay Diaries* 145.

[13] *Douay Diaries* 148.

On 15 July 1621 Drury's *Repartus S^{ti} Joannis Evangelistae* was performed "publice ac cum laude."[14] This lost play concerning the baptism of St. John is not to be confused with *Repartus sive Depositum*, the third and last surviving play of Drury's, which was first introduced in the edition of 1628.

A few weeks after the performance of the play about St. John, the Douai diarist records in a memorable phrase that Drury left the College, "in vinea Anglicana laborent."[15] Records of Drury's activities in England are sketchy. It is certain that on 26 October 1623 William's Jesuit brother, Robert, delivered the sermon at Hunsdon House in Blackfriars, London, on an occasion that proved to be tragic and highly publicized.[16] Between two and three hundred Catholics attended this extraordinary public convocation. Crowding into a third-floor room to hear the sermon, the congregation by its collective weight overtaxed the main beam, which collapsed, killing Robert Drury and at least ninety others.[17] Although William was believed to be among the dead, he escaped (if indeed he was in attendance, as seems likely); for when in 1631 his nephew, also named William Drury, perpetuated the family tradition by enrolling in the English College at Douai and adopting the alias of Bedford, Drury wrote a letter of commendation on his behalf.[18]

After serving as a confessor, William Drury was imprisoned in the Clink in 1632 and then in the New Prison in 1633.[19] This same Father Drury, identified as one jailed for "recusancy," was released from the Clink on 24 March 1635.[20] The fact that William's nephew suddenly left the College without permission on 15 May 1632, returning on 13 March 1633, suggests that the young man may have attempted to assist his uncle, but there is no way of knowing for sure.[21]

References to the priest-dramatist subsequent to his imprisonment cannot be trusted. The 1641 publication of Drury's works with the notation, "Editio *ultima* ab ipso authore recognita," suggests that by this date the dramatist-priest was indeed deceased.[22] An anti-papist pam-

---

14 *Douay Diaries* 185.

15 *Douay Diaries* 186.

16 Foley 1:77–98.

17 Foley 1:77.

18 Freeman, 295–96; *Douay Diaries* 293.

19 Anstruther, 88; Foley 1:279; 6:235.

20 *Calendar of State Papers, Domestic series, Charles I*, ed. John Bruce, 23 vols. (1864; repr., Nendeln, Lichtenstein: Kraus Reprints, 1967) 7:285; 587; Anstruther, 88–89.

21 *Douay Diaries* 304, 312; Sinconolfi, 24.

22 Emphasis mine. See Geoffrey Holt, *St. Omers and Bruges Colleges, 1593–1773, A Biographical Dictionary* (89); Freeman (296–97); and Siconolfi, 25–26.

phlet that Parliament ordered published in 1643 observing that a "Mr. Drury" was living as a member of a canonical chapter in Paris or Douai may not refer to the dramatist, since other Drurys were alive at this time, at least one of whom had been ordained.[23]

Drury's Literary Works

The first edition of Drury's plays, published in Douai in 1620, bears the title *Aluredus sive Alfredus Tragicomoedia ter exhibita, in seminario anglorum duaceno ab eiusdem collegii iuventute, anno Domini MDCXIX.* This edition also contains a second play, *Mors,* and a Latin poem entitled "De Venerabili Eucharistia." Whether the Douai diarist was referring to the comedy *Mors* or the tragicomedy *Aluredus* when he wrote that the "Comoediam" was acted "cum alacritate ac applausu"[24] is a matter of dispute, since the diarist distinguishes between comedies and tragicomedies in several other entries.[25] What is indisputable is that *Aluredus* takes pride of place in the printed edition. The prefatory matter and elaborate dedication to Count Gondomar are all focused upon it, as is the title of the publication. Additionally, the list of *errata* at the end of the volume corrects only the mistakes in *Aluredus.*[26] These considerations suggest that *Aluredus* may originally have been the sole work intended for publication.

The 1628 edition, also printed in Douai, bears the more impressive title, *Dramatica Poemata. Authore D. Guilielmo Druraeo Nobili Anglo. Editio secunda ab ipso authore recognita, & multo quam prima auctior reddita.* By this date Drury had made a name for himself, and the publisher was trading on it. The augmented edition reprints *Aluredus* and *Mors* and adds the tragicomedy *Reparatus sive Depositum,* presumably composed between 1620 and 1628. The final edition, published in Douai and Antwerp, in 1641, omits the dedication to Count Gondomar, which by this date would have been not only outdated but inflammatory with respect to its matter, especially given the anti-papist feeling in the country. The type, it may also be noted, has been recast, and since the author evidently was not present to oversee the production, the edition contains many gross misprints. In all other respects, however, the content of the 1641 edition is the same as that of the 1628 edition.

Among his select readership, *Mors* is roundly attested to be the best

---

[23] Holt, 89; Dominic A. Bellenger, ed., *English and Welsh Priests 1558–1800* (Bath, England: Downside Abbey, 1984), 55.

[24] *Douay Diairies* 148.

[25] Siconolfi, 59.

[26] Siconolfi makes the point (84).

of Drury's plays, swiftly paced, admirably constructed, and thoroughly stageworthy.[27] *Mors* felicitously conjoins the stock characters of Latin comedy and the Commedia dell'Arte with those of the native dramatic tradition. The mixing of traditions permits the characters of the miserly *senex* (Chrysocancrio), the spendthrift son (Scombrio), the servant (Crancus), and *miles gloriosus* to confront the medieval dramatic characters of Death and the Devil, along with a sorceress thrown in for good measure, producing novel situations unknown in Plautine and Terentian comedy. Pleasingly ambitious is Drury's duplication of the Faustus motif whereby the dramatist has Scombrio make a pact to sell his body to Death and another to sell his soul to the Devil. By dramatizing both motifs but casting the greater emphasis upon the contract with Death, Drury displays an inventiveness that may be likened to Shakespeare's doubling of the pairs of identical twins in his Plautine extravaganza *The Comedy of Errors.*

The knockabout physical comedy in *Mors,* which includes witches' conjurations, the introduction of an ass's and a bull's head, and the theft of the Cook's food in a harp-case, brings the play closer to farce than to comedy. By contrast, *Reparatus, sive Depositum* belongs to pastoral tragicomedy. Like *Aluredus,* the play has a historical setting—Sardis during the reign of Domitian—and its well-worn, romantic action depicts female virtue in distress, as well as the separation and subsequent reunion of a shipwrecked family. Through its principal character, Reparatus, a repentent robber who converts to Christianity, *Reparatus* also manifests the didacticism and Senecan self-reflection characteristic of Jesuit academic drama.[28] Less well unified than either *Aluredus* or *Mors, Reparatus* introduces new plots and characters in the third and fourth acts, including a bishop of Sardis, who recounts the persecution of Christians under Domitian. The fifth act, which shows Drury continuing to mix his modes, presents an allegorical display of Despair and the Seven Deadly Sins, each of whom encourages Reparatus to commit suicide, a temptation the protagonist successfully resists by seizing the cross.

As this outline of events illustrates, Drury's extant plays show him to have been familiar with classical Roman comedy and tragedy, the medieval moralities, and the popular and learned dramatic traditions of the Elizabethan-Jacobean age. As an academic dramatist and a priest, Drury placed his knowledge of these traditions in the service of Catholic culture and pedagogy.

---

[27] Hall, 70–73; Siconolfi, 58–60, 89; Francis Douce, *Holbein's Dance of Death* (London: George Bell & Sons, 1884), 156.

[28] Ernest Boysse, *Le Théâtre des Jesuites* (1880; repr. Geneva: Slatkine Reprints, 1970), passim.

Drury's *Mors* was translated into English in the seventeenth century by Robert Squire as *Death, A Comedie*. The manuscript bears no date, but Squire's editor, observing the low percentage of italic graphs in the mixed secretary hand, suggests the 1630s, although this same evidence could be adduced to support a date as early as the 1620s.[29] Squire's own identity remains elusive, although the mention of a Father Edward Squire in the testimony of students at the English College in Rome in 1628 raises the possibility that Robert came from a devout Catholic family.[30] The notice immediately following the play's title, "Written in Latin by M. W. D. and translated into Engl*ish* by Rob*ert* Squire," shows that Squire wished to acknowledge his predecessor's work (even though he was reluctant to provide Drury's full name) and was attempting to bring it to a larger, English-speaking audience.[31]

From one perspective, Knightley's mid-seventeenth-century translation of *Aluredus* may be viewed as a parallel to Squire's earlier one, each evincing in its way Drury's long-lived reputation as a playwright. The translation of any such Neo-Latin play is rare in the seventeenth century;[32] the translation of two by the same author (under separate auspices) is, to my knowledge, unprecedented. From another vantage point, the translation of *Aluredus* may be of still greater cultural significance, for it shows concretely the continuity of the English Catholic tradition during the early Stuart period. When Knightley Englished *Aluredus* forty years after Drury had composed it and probably more than a generation after Squire had translated *Mors*, he was doing more than preserving a literary reputation or a cultural artifact; he was adapting and redirecting the political message of Drury's tragicomedy to the needs of royalist English Catholics, whose world had been placed in jeopardy by the Puritan revolution, the overthrowing of the monarchy, and the execution of Charles I.

The Translator, "R. K.," and the Dedicatee, "Lady Blounte"

The translator of *Alfrede or Right Reinthron'd* identifies himself only as "R. K." The Bodleian Library *Summary Catalogue*, which in no way indicates that the play is anything but original, shows the ratiocination that led to the "author's" identification: "the dedication to lady (Mary) Blount is signed by her brother 'R. K.' the author, who therefore ap-

[29] Siconolfi, 83–88.

[30] Foley 1:201; 6: 322; Siconolfi, 78–79.

[31] Siconolfi, 116.

[32] Siconolfi, 63.

pears to be a Kirkham."[33] Following this attribution, Harbage, Schoenbaum, and Wagonheim identify the playwright as "R. Kirkham (?)," otherwise "unknown."[34] All other references to the play follow this ascription.

The logic behind this identification is sound, but ironically it does not stand up to investigation. Inseparable from the question of the author's identity is that of the play's dedicatee, "ye Lady Blounte." The name of Blount provides the only firm starting point for our examination. Since the dedication is signed, "your most affectionate / Brother," the obvious deduction is that the dedicatee was married, that her maiden name was Kirkham (or at least began with a K), and that she had married into the Blount family. These latter inferences can be confirmed.

The social station of the translator's sister is that of a gentle lady. In the mid-seventeenth century, it is true, the term "lady" could be used as a decorous appellation; but the translator's emphatic use of "ye Lady Blounte" as a title, means that the sister is being addressed formally, in accord with the original meaning of the word, as the lady of a lord's household, and that her husband's status is at least that of a knight.[35] This analysis accords with the fact that the Blount name was a redoubtable one. The family's many strains included figures such as Sir Henry Blount (1602–1682) and the famous Mountjoy Blount (1597?–1666), who was the earl of Newport and the son of Charles Blount, earl of Devonshire by Lady Penelope Rich.[36]

To identify the dedicatee's family, it was necessary to discover a gentry lady whose surname was Kirkham (or at least began with "K") and who married into the Blount family before the signed date of "1659" found at the conclusion of the Alfrede manuscript. Genealogies show several Kirkhams and numerous propertied Blounts, but only one recorded marriage between a woman whose maiden name was Kirkham (or even began with "K") and a Blount. Croke's *Genealogical History of the Croke Family, Originally Named Le Blount* provides the following positive identification:

> The eldest son of Sir Walter Blount, the first Baronet, was SIR GEORGE BLOUNT, who married Mary, the sole daughter and

---

[33] *Summary Catalogue* 298.

[34] Alfred Harbage, *Annals of English Drama, 975–1700*, rev. S. Schoenbaum (1964); rev. 3d. ed., Sylvia S. Wagonheim (London and New York: Routledge, 1989), 156, 228.

[35] *The Compact Edition of the Oxford English Dictionary: Complete Text Reproduced Micrographically* (Oxford: Oxford Univ. Press, 1971), s.v. "lady"; Peter Laslett, *The World We Have Lost*, 3rd. ed. (New York: Charles Scribner's Sons, 1984), 38.

[36] *DNB*, s.v. "Blount."

> heiress of Richard Kirkham, of Blackdown, in Devonshire, son and heir to Sir William Kirkham, Knight, by his second wife, daughter of Sir—Tychburne. He [George Blount] died at Mawley, in 1667, and was buried at Mample. He had seven sons, and four daughters. Kirkham bore, argent, within a bordure ingrailed, sable, three lions rampant, gules, armed and langued, azure.[37]

This identification is corroborated by Prince's *The Worthies of Devon*, which records that Richard Kirkham of Blagdon "had issue Mary," who married "the Honourable Sir George Blunt of Sodington in Worcestershire, Baronet," and also by Polwhele's *History of Devonshire*, which preserves this information, adding that Mary brought to that family the ancestral Kirkham lands of Ashcombe and other lands as well.[38]

The dedicatee of the *Alfrede* manuscript is then Mary (Kirkham) Blount. From a noted landed family bearing a coat of arms, she married into a still more illustrious family that traces its lineage back to Blanche, the first wife of John of Gaunt in Richard II's time.[39] The problem, however, is not so much in identifying Mary but in piecing together her putative relationship to an unidentified blood brother, "R. K.": Croke, Prince, and Polwhele all record that Mary was Richard Kirkham's "sole" or "only daughter and heiress."[40]

Arguably, the description of Mary as "sole" or "only daughter and heiress" could imply that she had at least one brother who predeceased her father, thus enabling Mary to inherit. However, the phrase "only daughter and heiress" seems to function explanatorily: Mary was her father's only *child*, who therefore (despite her being a female) inherited substantial Kirkham lands. The will of Mary's father provides the most definitive evidence that can be had. Born in 1594, Richard Kirkham, heir to the estate of his father William Kirkham, Knight of Blagdon, died on 16 March 1630.[41] Probated on 8 July 1631, the will names Richard's two-year-old daughter, Mary Kirkham, as his heir.[42] In the context of the will, "sole daughter and heir" means

---

[37] Alexander Croke, *The Genealogical History of the Croke Family, Originally Named Le Blount*, 2 vols. (Oxford, 1823), 2:146.

[38] John Prince, *Danmonii Orientales Illustres: or, The Worthies of Devon* (1697; repr. London, 1810), 555; Richard Polwhele, *The History of Devonshire*, 3 vols. (1793–1806; repr. Dorking: Kohler & Coombes, 1977), 2:154; 3:491n.

[39] *Burke's Peerage and Baronetage*. 105th ed. (repr. London: Genealogical Books, 1970), 287–88; also Croke (2:381–82). Unless otherwise noted, birth, death, and marriage dates pertaining the Blount family are from *Burke's Peerage*.

[40] Croke 2:146; Prince, 555; Polwhele 3:491n.

[41] *Public Record Office. Inquisitions Post Mortem*. Chancery Series II, vol. 464, no. 23; and vol. 521, no. 120.

[42] *PRO, Inquisitions*, vol. 521, no. 120; *Visitations of the County of Devon*

"sole child" and heir. Additionally, the Kirkham family pedigree does not name any son of Richard Kirkham.[43] This information provides as much evidence as one can reasonably hope to have in attempting to prove the unprovable—someone's non-existence. In sum, the putative existence of "R. Kirkham" is a scholarly construct without a concrete foundation: Mary's brother "R. Kirkham" never lived.

If "R. Kirkham" never existed, who, then, could have signed himself to Mary Blount in 1659 as "your most affectionate / Brother"? Two possibilities present themselves: "brother" could describe a relation that is, more precisely, that of either a brother-in-law or a half-brother. Unlikely as the odds would seem to be, Mary had both a brother-in-law and a half-brother who could sign themselves "R. K."

Of George Blount's four sisters, the eldest, Eleanor, married "Rob. Knightley, esq. of Off-Church Co. Warwick."[44] This "R. K." was, however, an older man. Born in 1576, this brother-in-law of Mary's had been married twice before and late in life had married the young Eleanor, by whom he had two children.[45] He died in 1655 at the venerable age of seventy-nine, about five years before the making of *Alfrede,* and thus could not have been its translator.

Yet by an extraordinary circumstance, this in-law of the Blounts was also the father of the "R. K." who translated *Aluredus.* The Robert Knightley whose third wife was Eleanor Blount had lost his first wife, Anne Pettus of Norwich, in 1629.[46] Following Anne's death, the widower had remarried; and his second wife was Richard Kirkham's widow, Mary. The legal papers of 1635 settling Richard's estate comment that Mary in her widowhood had already taken the profits due her and had been remarried to Robert Knightley esquire of Worcester.[47]

Soon after her remarriage to Robert Knightley, Mary bore two children. The younger was named Valentine, the older, Robert, after his father.[48] The young Robert was thus Mary (Kirkham) Blount's half-brother on her mother's side. *This* Robert Knightley, the only "R.

Comprising the Heralds' Visitations of 1531, 1564, and 1620, ed. John L. Vivian (Exeter, 1895), 517.

[43] *Visitations, Devon* 517.

[44] Robert Douglas, *The Peerage of Scotland,* vol. 1 (Edinburgh, 1813), 127–28; Treadway Russell Nash, *Collections for the History of Worcestershire,* 3 vols. (London, 1781–82), 2:162a.

[45] K. T. Swanzy, *The Offchurch Story* (Abingdon, Berkshire: Abbey Press, 1968), 224.

[46] *The Visitation of the County of Warwick in the Year 1619* (taken by William Camden), ed. John Fetherston (London, 1877), 401; Swanzy, 65.

[47] *PRO, Inquisitions,* vol. 521, no. 120.

[48] *Douay Diairies* 521; Anstruther, 180.

K." in 1659–1660 who was also Mary's (half) brother, is the person who produced *Alfrede or Right Reinthron'd.*

Robert Knightley, the creator of *Alfrede,* is no cipher in the historical record. Probably born in the early years of his mother's second marriage—ca. 1632–1634—Robert was Mary (Kirkham) Knightley's next-born child after Mary Kirkham and was thus close in age to his half-sister. Although hard evidence is lacking, Mary Knightley probably brought her daughter with her to Off-Church when she remarried. If this deduction is correct, Mary grew up in Off-Church in the same household with her younger half-brothers.

However, by 1642, when Mary was about fourteen and Robert eleven or younger, their mother had died. With both her legal parents deceased, Mary Kirkham, according to a pedigree in Nash's *Collections for the History of Worcestershire,* was declared an "heir in ward."[49] She probably did not remain with her half-brothers at Off-Church a great deal longer, for within a few years of her mother's death, Mary, heiress to the Kirkham estate of Ashcombe,[50] was certainly married to Sir George Blount, himself the heir to Sir Walter Blount's estates.

The evidence for this reconstruction is strong. Although no record appears to have survived of the birth dates of George and Mary Blount's children, their eldest son and heir, Sir Walter Kirkham Blount (d. 1717), translated *The Office of the Holy Week* (Paris) in 1670. It seems reasonable to surmise that Sir Walter undertook this ambitious project after he had completed his formal education. If so, Sir Walter's birth year may be placed, roughly, at 1645—and almost surely not later than 1649. This would indicate that Mary Kirkham (who was born in 1628) almost surely left Off-Church to become Mary Blount before she had turned twenty-one and was by this time a mother. Indeed, at the time of the Restoration when Robert dedicated *Alfrede* to her, Mary may already have had all of the seven children born to her and George.[51]

Robert's own departure from Off-Church after his half-sister's marriage is revealed by a record from the English College at Douai showing that on 6 October 1652, Robert's father enrolled his two sons, "Robertus and Valentinus," in the College. Significantly, the diarist records that they had just arrived from Paris, were "armigeri" (i.e., the family bore a coat of arms), and had been "ab infantia suci in fide Catholica instructe et educate."[52] If normal practice was followed, as seems likely, the boys were enrolled while in their late teens. Our knowledge that Robert attended the English College at Douai is cru-

---

[49] Nash, 1:2a.

[50] Polwhele 2:154.

[51] Nash 2:162a.

[52] *Douay Diaries* 521.

cial, for it explains his proficiency in Latin, his familiarity with the highly literate, thoroughly English culture at Douai, as well as with Douai's dramatic traditions, and, one infers, his knowledge of William Drury's signal contributions to that tradition.

Unfortunately, a break in the *Douay Diaries* occurs from 1654 to 1676, so no further record pertaining to Robert or Valentine appears. Still, if Robert and Valentine remained in residence until completing the prescribed course of studies (exclusive of the advanced courses preparatory to the priesthood), they would have studied the classics and classical history and taken classes in rudiments, rhetoric, poetry, syntax, and grammar.[53] In the normal course of events, they would have returned to England in 1656 or 1657—two or three years before Robert translated *Aluredus.*

The years following the Restoration offer a relatively clear view of Robert Knightley's settling into life as a country gentleman and businessman. He is known to have married and to have had several daughters.[54] His brother Valentine, who never married, lived with him and eventually became his business partner.[55] Although not the heir to the Knightley estate—that was left to Sir John Knightley, eldest son of Robert Knightley, the "Recusant," by his first marriage[56]—Robert was a man of considerable means. In September 1660, the date of the death of his godfather, Andrew Knightley, a redoubtable priest, Robert inherited substantial lands in Stoneythorpe, Southam, Warwickshire and Ravenstone, Packington, Leicestershire.[57] Robert's land transactions are recorded as part of the history of Warwickshire and Worcestershire. In 1667 a rent from the manor of Bosworth's Farm in Warwickshire in the amount of 13 pounds, 6 shillings and 8 pence was conveyed by Robert Knightley and others to Robert Beale and John Poweil.[58] A year later Robert bought a parcel of land at North Piddle from Thomas Powis.[59] Robert's name and Valentine's appear in another transaction in 1683/84, in which the brothers conveyed land in

53 *Douay Diaries* xxix.

54 Swanzy, 65.

55 Swanzy, 65, 112.

56 *Visitation of Warwick* 401; Swanzy, 93–95.

57 Anstruther, 180, whose ultimate source is *Public Record Office, Probate Wills,* 300, fol. 188.

58 *Victoria History of the Counties of England: Warwickshire,* 8 vols. (Oxford Univ. Press for the Univ. of London Institute of Historical Research, 1904–69; repr., London: Dawsons of Pall Mall, 1965–69), 6:128.

59 *Victoria History of the Counties of England: Worcestershire,* 4 vols. (1901–24; repr. Folkestone & London: Dawsons of Pall Mall for the Univ. of London Institute of Historical Research, 1971), 4:179.

North Piddle to Thomas Yarnold.[60] Whether this last transfer of property was prompted by illness is not known, but in 1684 Robert Knightley died.[61]

The official nature of both the *Douay Diaries* and the records of Robert's business transactions preclude any personal revelation of Robert's interests or character. To glean something of these, we turn to Robert's dedication page in *Alfrede*. The tone is both respectful and intimate. The dedication shows Robert to be mindful of the formalities of addressing his eminent half-sister, whose husband had come into the Blount inheritance in 1654. Already a mother who had given birth to several children, including the next heir of the Blount fortune,[62] Mary was approximately thirty-two years of age in 1659–1660 and clearly at the center of the Blount family. At the same time, the dedication displays a welcome playfulness that reveals itself in Robert's conceit about his book being (like St. Neot, he implies) a recluse immured within his sister's cabinet. The formality and the playfulness come together in Robert's profession of admiration for his sister, which, like the whole of the dedication, has religious overtones: "devotion" impels him to present *Alfrede* as a "consecrated" "Offering" (lines 11–12).

A darker side is revealed in Robert's confession that he composed *Alfrede* to ward off melancholy. We may wonder whether the melancholy was of a purely personal sort, or was tied to the social themes of the play he translated. Certainly his playful notion that thoughts not wed to their proper objects are "schismaticall" (Ded., line 4) reveals an acute awareness of the dangers engendered by religious heterodoxy. So too, the Epilogue, the only place where Robert actively reworks his source, discloses the translator's concern with the fate of his country, a concern that may reasonably be linked to Robert's allusions to his "entervalls of externe cogitations" as well as his self-confessed need "of passing away the time" (Ded., lines 3–4, 7). Sparse as these autobiographical details are, they reveal an educated, polished, well-connected country gentleman who worked comfortably with his Latin play-text. At a somewhat deeper level, they disclose an affectionate, witty, reflective, and even brooding brother whose piety and Catholic allegiances are manifest in the play he translated.

---

[60] *History, Worcestershire* 4:179.

[61] Swanzy, 112.

[62] Nash 2:162a.

Alfrede and the English Catholic Community

The foregoing account of the genesis of *Alfrede* looks to individuals; it provides one kind of explication. But to appreciate the larger significance of the transmission of *Aluredus* it is necessary look to the familial and institutional forces that fostered the English reincarnation of Drury's play as *Alfrede or Right Reinthron'd.* To peruse these is to illuminate the intricate network of institutional connections and shared cultural experiences by which the rural Catholic gentry generated a cohesive identity and sustained itself through a half century of oppression.

Mary Blount's family of origin is a good place to begin. In order for her to marry into the illustrious Blount family, the religious affiliations and reputation of Mary's own family would have counted heavily. The fact that Mary brought to her marriage substantial, ancient landholdings has already been shown.[63] But Kirkham lands alone were insufficient to seal such an important match. The family's prominence in the West country and its history as a leading Catholic family in the shire were also crucial.[64]

Several converging pieces of evidence illustrate the strength of the Kirkhams' Catholic allegiances. In 1639, four years after the settling of Mary's father's estate, Mary's uncle, Francis Kirkham, who had received Pinhoe as the eldest surviving brother, and his wife, Elizabeth, were presented for recusancy.[65] Their attachment to Catholicism was no isolated expression of religious conviction. William Kirkham of Devonshire (b. ca. 1594), evidently the third-eldest brother, was a Jesuit who worked on the English mission before his death in 1624;[66] and the family's commitment continued unflaggingly. Richard Kirkham's uncles Giles (1607–1631) and Robert (b. 1609) were enrolled in the English College at Douai in August 1624.[67] Although Giles had to leave the College prematurely because of illness ("corpore infirmus"), his brother stayed the full course, earning the title of "theologus" in 1631.[68] Giles and Robert were thus at the English College when Drury's name was current, and Robert was still studying there when

[63] Polwhele 2:154.

[64] Polwhele 2:31.

[65] Oliver, George and J. P. Jones, *Ecclesiastical Antiquities of Devon, Being Observations of Many Churches in Devonshire,* 3 vols. (Oxford & New York: Oxford Univ. Press, 1985), 2:126.

[66] *The English College at Valladolid: Registers, 1589–1862,* ed. E. Henson, Catholic Record Society, vol. 30 (London: John Whitehead & Son, 1930), 113.

[67] *Douay Diaries* 230.

[68] *Douay Diaries* 236, 296.

the 1628 edition of Drury's plays was published at Douai. Although Robert Knightley did not dedicate his *Alfrede* to these Kirkhams, their history as alumni of the English College obviously constitutes a part of Mary's family heritage and of the cultural context in which *Alfrede* was translated and dedicated.

If we go on to examine the religious allegiances of the family into which Mary married, the family's connection to the English College at Douai is so strong as to be startling. The patriarch of the family, Mary's father-in-law, Sir Walter Blount, baronet, was a provincial Catholic leader of very substantial standing. When Dr. Matthew Kellison, longtime president of the English College (since 1613), was constrained to leave Douai because of the virulence of the plague, he fled to England. The place where he found refuge was the home of Sir Walter Blount. At Sodington, Sir Walter hosted Kellison for three years, from 1636 to 1639, until his guest could resume his duties at Douai.[69] Such an extended commitment highlights the eminence of the Blounts as a provincial Catholic family; it also dramatizes the general truth that "The ability of English gentry to offer the necessary protection to the outlawed priests ... [and Catholic educators was] a crucial element in the revival of catholicism" in the late sixteenth and early seventeenth centuries.[70]

Sir Walter Blount's relationship to Kellison's College at Douai endured. On 14 July 1642, Sir Walter and his wife enrolled their fifteen year-old son, Thomas, at the College.[71] Significantly, the Douai diarist describes Thomas's parents as "amborum Catholicorum," and Thomas himself as "natus in comitatu Wigorniensi [Worcestershire] in Catholica religione ab incunabulis educatus."[72] Other records show that Sir Walter entered Thomas and another son, named Edward, at St. Omer's.[73]

The Catholic heritage of the Knightley family of Off-Church, Warwickshire was equally formidable. Its chief figure, Robert's long-lived father, attained the sobriquet of "the Recusant."[74] This is the same gentleman who entered the Blount family late in life by marrying Eleanor, Mary (Kirkham) Blount's sister-in-law. These inter-marriages

---

[69] *Douay Diaries* 489, 542.

[70] Alan Dures, *English Catholicism 1558–1642: Continuity and Change* (Essex, England: Longman, 1983), 24, 69. Cf. Edward Norman, *Roman Catholicism in England from the Elizabethan Settlement to the Second Vatican Council* (Oxford & New York: Oxford Univ. Press, 1985), 31.

[71] Holt, 39; *Douay Diaries* 436.

[72] *Douay Diaries* 436.

[73] Holt, 39.

[74] Swanzy, 224.

whereby Robert became Mary Blount's stepfather and then her brother-in-law, are the result, one suspects, of a close-knit Catholic gentry community in which marital opportunities were limited. Not surprisingly, Bridget, the elder Robert's daughter by his marriage to Anne Pettus, was presented for recusancy in 1633.[75] The elder Robert's sister Elizabeth became a nun at Lisbon, and his sister Dorothy joined the order of Poor Clare.[76] Both surviving brothers of the recusant, Edward and Andrew, were closely identified with Catholicism. Although not a priest, Edward devoted nine years, from 1600 to 1609, to his studies at the English Colleges at St. Omer's and Valladolid.[77] Edward's son John, the family pedigree shows, became a Benedictine monk, and Edward's brother Andrew rose to become the papal vicar-general.[78] From his return to Warwickshire as a priest in 1632 until his death in 1660, Andrew Knightley rose steadily in prominence; in 1653 he was appointed collector for London as well as Middlesex, where he was made a religious capitular in 1654.[79] Significantly, this papal official bequeathed the very substantial sum of fifty pounds to the College at Douai and to the religious order at Lisbon as well as to the chapter.[80] His strong connection with Douai can be seen as revealing another dimension to his godson Robert's own association with the College in the 1650s. In addition to extensive property, Andrew Knightley bequeathed to his godson-nephew, of whom he must have been fond, a personal remembrance—his gold seal ring.[81]

A still more expansive picture of the Knightley family's religious heritage comes into view from surveying the history of the shire. Off-Church or Off-Churchbury was the manorial seat of the Knightleys, and like the Kirkham and Blount estates in Devonshire and Worcestershire, it was ancestral.[82] So staunchly Catholic were the Knightleys that *The Victoria History of Warwick* commences its account of Roman Catholicism in the county with an examination of the Knightley clan at Off-Church.[83] Because of the family's Catholicism, the Off-Church estate was taken over by the crown in 1626 and leased to one John Pecke for twenty-one years.[84] Nonetheless, this branch of the family

---

[75] Swanzy, 65–66.
[76] Anstruther, 179.
[77] *English College, Valladolid* 89; Holt, 155–56.
[78] Swanzy, 224.
[79] Anstruther, 179–80.
[80] Anstruther, 180.
[81] Swanzy, 65.
[82] *History, Warwickshire* 6:195–96.
[83] *History, Warwickshire* 8:368.
[84] *History, Warwickshire* 6:196.

remained Roman Catholic until Sir John Knightley, second baronet and heir, turned to Anglicanism sometime before his death in 1688, when, ironically, the direct male line died out.[85]

An entry in the register of the English College at Valladolid suggests the kind of social connections the Knightleys enjoyed among Catholics at the national level. On the day that Edward Knightley of Off-Churchbury was admitted to the English College at Valladolid, 15 October 1606, the diarist described Edward, aged eighteen, as the scion of noble English Catholic parents, and reported that the young man entered with the "comẽndatione P. Garneti [Henry Garnett] et P. Olcorne [Edward Oldcorne]."[86] These were the priests most closely associated with the Gunpowder Plot of 5 November 1605, for which they were immediately imprisoned and Garnett examined twenty-three times before the Privy Council.[87] Edward Knightley thus appeared at Valladolid with commendations from England's two most spectacularly martyred Jesuits, and within six and a half months of their torture and spectacular executions in May of 1606.[88]

These strong links of the Kirkhams, Blounts, and Knightleys to Douai and other continental Catholic colleges may be seen as symptomatic of the Catholic gentry's alienation from England's national church, but not as simple disloyalty to England. Even though they were labelled traitors when they attempted to rear their children in the Catholic faith, they were, from their traditionalist's perspective, attempting to preserve their country's ancient religion, with its heritage of saints, from what they believed, or hoped, was the aberration of a state-run church independent of Rome.[89] Furthermore, almost all were loyal to the crown and acknowledged its authority in temporal matters. Seeing themselves as English and Catholic both, many gentry families sent their children to what were after all *English* colleges on the Continent. In so doing, they faced extensive anti-Catholic property and penal laws, laws against the inculcation of Catholic beliefs, and severe restrictions, however desultorily enforced, on public worship.[90]

Most Catholic families, like Anglican and Puritan ones, attempted to

---

85 Anstruther, 179; see *History, Warwickshire* 8:368.

86 *English College, Valladolid* 89.

87 *DNB*, s.v. "Garnett"; Anstruther, 138, 154.

88 See G. P. V. Akrigg's colorful account of the plot in *Jacobean Pagant or the Court of James I* (1962; repr. New York: Athenaeum, 1974), 74–76 and Philip Caraman's exhaustive one of Father Garnet and the plot in *Henry Garnet, 1555–1606 and the Gunpowder Plot* (London: Longmans, 1964).

89 Dures, 36.

90 Norman, 32–56; John Miller, *Popery and Politics in England, 1660–1688* (Cambridge: Cambridge Univ. Press, 1973), 51–58.

preserve a safe neutrality when the civil war broke out, but remaining neutral was made difficult by parliamentarian lawmakers who repeatedly passed legislation equating Roman Catholicism with royalism.[91] Not all Catholic families were nudged toward royalism, however; a number of leading Catholic families came out early in active support of the king.[92] Among them were the Kirkhams, the Blounts, and the Knightleys.

The records of the families involved in the making and transmission of *Alfrede* all attest to their royalism and to the hardships they endured. Of the Kirkhams, Polwhele says, "This family being Papists, had their estates sequestered, and suffered greatly in other respects during the grand rebellion and the protectorate."[93] Sir Walter Blount, for his part, risked virtually everything fighting for King Charles. Along with all his brothers and four of his sons, who took leadership roles in Charles's regiments, Sir Walter served with dedication.[94] "[A] zealous supporter of the king," he was captured in 1645, suffered imprisonment at Oxford and then in the Tower, and was subsequently fined heavily as a "Papist delinquent."[95] Papist delinquents—defined as those who fought on the king's behalf—were supposed to lose four-fifths of their lands, although many were able to avoid the full effects of the penalty through negotiation.[96] Blount's home at Sodington was "burnt" by Cromwell's troops when Sir Walter refused to allow them to make arms at his forge, and in 1652 all his estates were ordered confiscated.[97] His son and heir, Sir George Blount, recovered the family manor at the Restoration.[98]

Sir Walter Blount, who died in August 1654 and is interred at Paignton, Devonshire, did not live to see this event.[99] His wife, who died in 1656, is buried in the Blount Chapel in Mamble Church where tablets of many family members may be found.[100] By 1660 his daughter-in-law Mary (Kirkham) Blount, her husband, and their children had become the new center of the Blount family. Sir Walter's religious legacy devolved to them and was perpetuated most notably in Mary

---

[91] Keith Lindley, "The Part Played by the Catholics," *Politics, Religion and the English Civil War*, ed. Brian Manning (London: Edward Arnold, 1973), 126–30; Norman, 35–37.

[92] Norman, 35–36.

[93] Polwhele 2:31.

[94] Croke 2:145.

[95] *History, Worcestershire* 4:287.

[96] Miller, 9.

[97] Croke 2:145.

[98] *History, Worcestershire* 4:287.

[99] *Burke's Peerage* 287.

[100] *History, Worcestershire* 4:288–89.

and George's eldest son, Sir Walter Kirkham Blount, who translated *The Office of the Holy Week According to the Missal and Roman Breviary* (1670) and composed *The Spirit of Christianity* (1686) for James II. Such a family history illustrates the active role played by the Blount family in the maintenance of a nationalistic English Catholicism in the seventeenth century as well as the appropriateness of Robert Knightley's presenting his sister with his Anglo-Catholic Alfred play when he did.

The imprint of the civil war and of Douai upon Robert Knightley himself must not be forgotten either. The atmosphere in which he and Valentine had been admitted to the College had been charged. The *Diaries* are full of narratives of the persecutions and martrydoms that had occurred as a result of the civil wars and of Parliament's anti-papist legislation.[101] Both sons must have been mindful of the fact that their father was risking heavy penalties in daring to give his sons a Catholic education.[102] The times were also notorious for the number of spies they bred. Since some even "wormed their way into the College itself," the precautionary alias of "Parker" that Robert and his brother took upon entering was more than a formality.[103]

Against these great risks, there were some countervailing benefits. Just two years before Robert's enrollment at Douai, Charles II had visited the College.[104] In so doing he was demonstrating his appreciation for the sacrifices loyal Catholics had made on his behalf and, more shrewdly, his understanding that their support was instrumental in his plans to regain his throne. This event too is part of the context in which Knightley made his translation.

To consider the relationships among William Drury, the College at Douai where his plays were presented, Robert Knightley, the English translator of *Aluredus*, his prominent dedicatee Mary (Kirkham) Blount, and the Blount family is to recognize that the transmission of *Aluredus* and its English reincarnation as *Alfrede* cannot be properly explicated by piecemeal identifications. The history of *Aluredus* and *Alfrede* is, as I have said, a rare, concrete example of the transmission of Catholic recusant high culture and ideology. Even apart from the ideological content of the Alfred play, the acts of presenting, publishing, translating, and dedicating it all constitute a declaration of faith, whereby England's greater Catholic gentry, despite its minority status, reaffirmed its cultural identity and religion at home and abroad.

---

[101] *Douay Diaries* 432, 437, 440, 447; cf. Anstruther, 180.

[102] *Douay Diaries* xxviii.

[103] *Douay Diaries* xxviii, 521.

[104] *Douay Diaries* 505.

The Translation

Since the substantive content of *Aluredus* is the same in the 1620, 1628, and 1641 editions of the play (despite the notable misprints in the last), it is not possible to determine with any certainty which edition Knightley used to make his translation. However, two circumstances point to the 1641 edition. The first is simply that it was made closest in time to Knightley's translation. The second is that Knightley's work conjoins Act 4, scene 17 and Act 4, scene 18 into a single scene. This appears to be accidental inasmuch as the scene following is numbered 19 as if Knightley was not aware of the conflation. An explanation for this apparent oversight appears ready to hand when the 1620 and 1628 editions are compared with the recast 1641 edition. In the earlier editions "SCENA XVIII" appears prominently in the middle of the printed page, but in the 1641 edition the scene marker appears in a cramped position very near the bottom of the page. Following the heading there appears a one-and-one-half-line argument—"*Regina ab Osberno, & Gormone, coniectis in fugam latronibus, liberatur*" (70)—which Knightley, as is his custom throughout, does not translate. In addition, the scene heading is misspelled "SECNA XVIII." But prominently placed at the top of the next page is the list of characters for the scene, Osbernus, Gormo, and Edelvitha. Using a marginal stage direction, Knightley acknowledges the entrance of the two men, thereby commencing what is really another scene. It thus appears plausible that Knightley, using the 1641 edition, overlooked the defective end-of-page heading "SECNA XVIII" and simply continued the seventeenth scene by recording the new entrances noted at the top of the page. While certainly not conclusive, the hypothesis that Knightley *overlooked* the heading for scene eighteen because of its placement in the 1641 edition is consistent with the evidence.

In any case, Knightley's English translation of *Aluredus* follows the Latin text scene-for-scene and idea-for-idea. In the one other place where two scenes are conjoined—5.11 and 5.12 in *Aluredus* become 5.11 in *Alfrede* (in this case the subsequent scenes are correctly renumbered)—all the lines of dialogue are conscientiously preserved. Knightley's is, then, a close translation of *Aluredus,* but it is not slavish. Knightley renders the original Latin with fresh English dialogue and images. He also turns Drury's Latin trimeter, or iambic senarius verse as it is sometimes called—which has the effect of a six-foot iambic line to the ear of a native speaker of English—into English blank verse.

Perhaps the term "blank verse" is too exalted to describe the translation of *Alfrede.* At the least, it may be said that Knightley employs a ten-syllable line. Sometimes one feels that he is counting syllables mechanically: "Nor did the Nightingall, that Syren of / of the wood[,] chant forth its sweet Melodies" (2.1.74–75). In this passage, the preposition "of" mistakenly appears twice, once in each line, and yet in each case the word is needed to fill out the decasyllabic count. Despite this obvious limitation, the diction *is* poetic. This particular passage continues descriptively with melodramatic emphasis:

Nor any bird broke silence with a Note;
when a suddain horror invests the place;
A dreadfull tempest from the clouded North
benights the day: light'ning broke thorow
the condensed clouds; thunder (mixt wth raine)
Not much vnlike a Cannon furrowed
the ground, and shoke the Center of ye earth (2.1.76–82)

Since *Alfrede* was originally an academic play composed in Latin by a professor of rhetoric, it is not surprising to find a degree of pedantry in it. The play's mythological allusiveness, philosophical homiletic, and artificial formal dialogue are all part of the pattern. Knightley's close translation preserves these features even to the point of becoming entrapped by the original diction, as when Knightley renders Drury's "Caliginosis concutit" as the scarcely English "Caliginous clouds" (3.5.5).[105] Knightley's characters also express themselves unflinchingly in a language that even erudite clerics might well eschew, as when Osberne asks, "Shall we . . . / . . . terminate our quarrell, / or else go on with our incepted worke" (3.6.112–14).

Knightley is not above introducing awkward, Latinate images of his own. When he has Alfrede speak of fortune's "proteous vicissitude" (2.3.4), he creates a pedantic image not present in *Aluredus*. He occasionally becomes entangled in unaccommodating syntactic patterns suggested by the Latin original as well. A good example of this appears in the opening lines of the soliloquy in which Alfredus reflects on his misfortunes:

Agitata curis imperia quisquis colit,
Et credit omne positum in aurato decus
Fulgore sceptri, nec timet rerum vices;
Videat Britanni Regis Alvredi fugam. (2.3.1–4)

Knightley translates this as,

Who makes a Crowne, beset with thornes of Cares,
His Idoll and fancies the splendor of his scepter
the lookinglasse of all glory; nor feares
the proteous vicissitude of ffortune:

[105] Citations are from Hall's edition of Drury's *Aluredus*, the only one that provides line numbers. These citations also work as references to the printed editions, which offer act and scene divisions only.

Let Alfrede, once King of England, be his
Obiect . . . (2.3.1–6)

The construction "Who makes . . . and fancies . . . nor feares: . . . Let Alfrede" follows Drury's. Tortured as this syntax is, with its suspended introduction of Alfrede as subject and its negation after the initial, complex relative clause, the construction is grammatically correct. The result is a translation more elevated and ornate, and occasionally more strained in the serious passages than Drury's original. At its best, Knightley's verse attains a lofty, stiff formality as the main characters, following Drury, speak their bookish thoughts and work through their problems in the Senecan manner of philosophical debate. Such verse *is* appropriate to Alfred's station; it does communicate a sense of Alfred's misery along with the homiletic point, and it effectively reproduces the grandiloquence and "energeia" that were a hallmark of the Senecan revival.[106] Dutiful though it is, the translation also has its own afflatus, is usually on a par with Drury's original, and whether intentional or not, captures in its own idiom the studied Latinate texture of the serious scenes as well as the colloquial vigor of the comic ones.

Knightley's versification also shows variety. For example, his unrhymed ten-syllable line, which predominates in the body of the play, is set off from St. Cuthbert's rhymed couplets in the Prologue and Epilogue. Knightley also establishes poetic decorum by composing scenes in prose for the low-life characters. These scenes contain some of the most natural, idiomatic, and engaging dialogue the translation offers. Consider the following passage: "Here I haue bread, boyl'd fishes, and a Cup of stingo, I haue also flesh; butter and Cheese; if any of you are a hungry, or desire to sharpen his wit with good liquor, so that he be'nt a Dane, let him follow me to the taverne" (2.4.44–48). Here the everyday images are Drury's while the colloquialisms are Knightley's, as is the invocation of the "Cup of stingo."

Knightley's abilities as a translator are most fully realized in those comic passages in which colloquialism and high spirits dominate. Among the most memorable are the scenes in which Strumbo, the saucy adolescent, appears beside his toothless, virago mother, whose main pedagogical tools are invective and the rod. The farce of physical

[106] On matters of Senecan style, see G. K. Hunter, "Seneca and English Tragedy," in *Seneca*, ed. C. D. N. Costa (London and Boston: Routledge & Kegan Paul, 1974), 192–97; on Senecan "senteniae" and the "grandiose style," see J. W. Binns "Seneca and Neo-Latin Tragedy in England," in *Seneca*, ed. C. D. N. Costa (London and Boston: Routledge & Kegan Paul, 1974), 230.

abuse crackles with realism as Strumbo imagines the itch his buttocks will feel after he is "flea'd with rods in pisse" (2.7.7) for getting drunk. Still better is Strumbo's irrepressible gaminess, which allows him to overcome Crabula's threats with a show of gold, exposing his mother's greed and turning her contumacious barrages to sweet orisons. His moment of triumph, in which, following Seneca's *Thyestes* at the opening of the fifth act, he feels himself walking with his head above the clouds, is as exultant as it is vainglorious:

> Ho! Victory victory, victory! I haue won ye day. Now I walke aboue the thundring clouds, and thrust my head amongst the Stars. Tis enough to subdue an enimy; tis noble to shew Clemency to the conquered; where to you, mother, I deliver my Money, but to be kept for me. (2.8.32–36)

Several of Knightley's most zestful passages also manage to redirect the Senecan concentration of the original to comic ends. One splendid instance of this is the translation of Gothurnus's herodlike, serio-comic exasperation—"Fugitisque haud tandem meas/ Fugietis iras, ô nimis patiens furor" (3.14.3–4)—as, simply, "O too too patient in my Anger!" (3.14.6). With similar verve Knightley translates Titmus's apprehension that Bragadocia "Iactarit se me comesturum cum aceto quasi haleculam" (5.2.28) as Bragadocia's boast that "he would eat me vp with veneger like pickeld herring" (5.2.27–28). And again, Crabula's speech, "Quem si deprehendero semel profecto faciam / Ut huius et loci et temporis meminerit probe" (2.7.17–18) is raised to dramatic spectacle: "If once I find him out[,] I'll make him[—] he shall remember it as long as he liues" (2.7.21–22). This technique of spontaneous self-interruption is Knightley's, and it works well to convey Crabula's comical exasperation at not being able to find her son, whom she is intent on thrashing.

Apart from enlivening passages in which Drury's country characters figure prominently, Knightley's most important contribution appears in the stage directions, which are almost wholly absent in *Aluredus*. Partially fulfilling this function in Drury's text, however, is an "argument," or summary, that appears before each scene. Without these notations, readers would not even know (directions for stage business aside) what non-speaking characters are present in a given scene. Knightley's *Alfrede* systematically provides both kinds of directions in the marginalia at the precise points where they are needed. Ironically then, the Englished *Alfrede* has the virtue of realizing more completely than the original the play's theatricality. Indeed, it is likely that there would be fewer doubting observations about the actability of *Aluredus* if critics were reading Drury's play in its English translation. This concern for staging indicates that *Alfrede*, closet drama though it may seem, could well have been intended for private performance before Catholic friends at the Blount estate at Sodington.

Knightley's *Alfrede* abounds with calls for stage props as well. As with *Mors,* these require no extraordinary resources. *Alfrede* specifies the fixed props of a tree (in separate plots for three different sets of characters), a pit, and a point of exit to serve as Gothurnus's fifth-act retreat "*into a Castle*" (8.4). The conduct of stage business, as Knightley envisions it, calls for a king's regalia, including robes and a crown, a beggar's, a soldier's and a hermit's habit, a rope for binding, a wallet, a purse, gold, "a bag of money," a challenge letter, a cup of ale, a loaf of bread, a caudle, periwigs, a dagger, and several swords.

These directions are notable for their explicit designation of character movement—"*Bra: lookes for a place to hide himselfe in*" (3.4.60)—and their use of stage props—"*Pim: gets into yͤ tree*" (3.4.45). The directions are also vivid—"*Bra: seeing the Knife vpon yͤ ground starts back*" (3.5.41); inventive—"*Pim: pulls him out by yͤ heeles*" (3.15.26); and dramatically exuberant—"*[Gothurnus] runs at Osb: and gor: they pull of their periwigs*" (5.14.103). Considered together, they amount to more than a tidying up of Drury's text; they are a realization of the play's dramatic possibilities, and they show an imaginative alertness to the play in performance.

One means of measuring Knightley's imaginative powers is to observe his handling of the conventionalized echo scene in the third act. A literal translation would destroy the artistic effect of the original. But to invest the scene with rhymes in English requires technical skill and resourcefulness. Knightley solved this difficulty by creating a new set of terms that could serve as the echo words while still fulfilling the scene's strategic purpose of warning Edward that his sister's life is in danger:

> Thou invisible goddesse of the woods
> be propitious and tell me where
> Of my lost sister Elfrede I shall heare[.]
> *Eccho*:—Here
> Ist in this place then that my sister is[?]
> *Eccho*:—yes
> What to regaine her must I vndergoe?
> *Eccho*:—goe
> You bid me goe but say not whither.
> *Eccho*:—hither.
> How may I yet secure her from all harme?
> *Eccho*:—arme.
> Is there any one she's Prisoner to?
> *Eccho*:—two

Tis soe two Danes haue then surpris'd her.
Eccho:—priz'd her.
Prize they her[,] yet detain her 'gainst her will[?]
Eccho:—ill
A ffoes Loue soone Chastity divorceth.
Eccho: forceth
O Gods! And doth shee not with griefe abound?
Eccho:—bound.
Can Heau'n with so great wickednes accorde?
Eccho: A Corde.
Bound with a Corde? Why make I these delayes?
Ile either perish with her or vndoe it.
exit
Eccho: doe it. (3.1.23–49)

The most dramatically effective of the echo responses are the ones that do more than simply repeat the final word of the question. In response to Edward's fear of "harme," Eccho's injunction to "arme" is perhaps the most original rhyme in the set. The surprising contrast in tonality between the terms "abound" and "bound" and "accorde" and "A Corde" creates a strikingly somber effect. So too Eccho's responses throughout the scene promote a sense of mournful apprehensiveness. In this respect the scene compares favorably with the similarly lugubrious echo scene in *The Duchess of Malfi* (5.3), in which *all* of Echo's responses repeat the last words of the speaker.

The academic's hand is evident, however, in the use of "two" as the echo for "to," and "heare" for "here" inasmuch as both pairs of words are distinguishable only by spelling. Although "hither" and "wither" are genuine rhymes, the aspirate "h" in the first word cannot truly function as an echo of the quite different semivowel "wh" in "whither." And the answer of "yes" to "is" is strained. But Knightley's wit, evident in his dedication, is also at work here. He ends the scene with a fine poetic touch, having Edward, who hears that Elgine is "Bound with a Corde," vow to "vndoe it." Still better is Eccho's affirmative answer, "doe it."

Date

The inscription "1659" at the conclusion of *Alfrede* would appear to provide a definitive completion date for the manuscript. But since the dating system Knightley would have used is old style, the play could have been transcribed in its present final form anytime from 25 March 1659 to 24 March 1660. The question is, precisely when.

Since the celebratory conclusion seems calculated to anticipate

Charles's restoration, which was marked by his triumphal entry into London on 29 May 1660, Knightley probably brought his project to conclusion in early 1660. The certainty that Charles Stuart would be England's king was surely felt by 5 May 1660, when a motion asserting that the constitution resided in the king and the two houses of Parliament was passed without dissent. The Declaration of Breda, 4 April 1660, in which Charles spelled out his willingness to allow Parliament to determine the exceptions to the general amnesty he proposed, went far toward thwarting continued opposition. For Catholics too, the Declaration augured well, since the king declared in it that "no man shall be disquieted or called into question for differences of opinion in matter [*sic*] of religion which do not disturb the peace of the kingdom."[107] In addition, the loyalty and sacrifices of Catholics during the Civil War, not to mention their crucial role in assisting Charles in his escape from England, gave them very good reason in 1660 to expect that the re-enthroned king would pursue a policy of toleration for Catholics.[108] Perhaps he would eventually restore England to the Catholic faith.

Yet Charles's restoration could not have been assured too much before this time, and certainly not before the full import of the readmission of the excluded members, who were predominantly royalist, to Parliament on 21 February 1660. To an astute observer the direction of things could not have been very clear before March. The riots of the London apprentices, the gradual descent into chaos after Richard Cromwell's fall in September 1659, the inability of any elected body to maintain control of either the country or the army, and the inscrutability of General Monck, the only figure who in any sense could be said to be England's chief executive, all clouded England's prospects early in 1660. Although Charles's return was rumored on and off throughout 1659 and early 1660, royalist fortunes rose and fell precipitously during this extraordinary time.[109] Clarendon's *State Papers,* which treats the period from 1659 to May 1660 in over five hundred pages, reveals that rumors of Charles's imminent return from exile were rife from early April of 1659.[110] In fact, preparations for a rebellion stirred royalist hopes through the spring and early summer. Leaders of the royalist resistance groups the Sealed Knot and the Great Trust were in constant touch with the king. The plan was to coordinate a

---

[107] Kenyon, J. P., ed., *The Stuart Constitution, 1603–1688: Documents and Commentary* (Cambridge: Cambridge Univ. Press, 1966), 158.

[108] Norman, 37; Miller, 96–98.

[109] J. R. Jones, *Country and Court: England, 1658–1714* (London: Edward Arnold, 1978), 113–39; *Calendar of the Clarendon State Papers,* 5 vols., ed. F. J. Routledge (Oxford: Clarendon Press, 1932), 4:210, 215, 275, 285, 327, 363.

[110] *Calendar, Clarendon Papers* 4:172.

general rising in July with the king's return from the continent;[111] but plagued by Sir Richard Willys's betrayal and a lack of field leadership the rising was delayed until August.

The Blounts of Sodington and the main branch of the Kirkhams were located in Devonshire, in the west, one of only a few areas where the royalists enjoyed considerable gentry support. Charles had planned to land in Bristol, in the county adjacent to Devonshire. Although Devonshire as a whole was Parliamentarian and Puritan in sympathy during the Civil War, the county harbored noted royalists who were active in the king's cause.[112] When the belated and ill-fated rising did take place, the result for royalist supporters, both Catholic and non-Catholic, was ignominious. Many counties failed to rise, and several leaders quailed. When Sir George Booth resolutely decided to march on with his modest army in Cheshire, he lacked coordinated support from other counties, thus became an easy target, and was routed on 19 August by the able Commonwealth general George Lambert. Charles, learning of the thwarted rebellion, abandoned his plan to sail to England.[113]

The abortive rising naturally dampened royalist hopes for months; but it hardly extinguished them. So fractured and ineffective had Richard Cromwell's regime become and so fearsome did the army appear (clamoring for wages long in arrears) that royalists and moderates alike, along with commoners in the west and in fact throughout the countryside, continued to look to Charles Stuart as England's only feasible prospect for stability.

It was against this backdrop of failure and self-doubt (after August 1659), but also of continued anticipation of Charles II's return, I suggest, that Robert Knightley set about translating Drury's *Alfrede.*

A 1660 date for the completion of Knightley's project can be gleaned from the epilogue. Remarkably, this is the only place where Knightley suppresses a part of Drury's play, the entire second half of the epilogue. At the same time, Knightley refocuses the emphasis of the opening lines. Why should he have done this? In the omitted passage Drury's St. Cuthbert calls upon his fellow Catholics to continue the struggle against England's heretical religion, but to do so by acts of prayer and suffrance rather than violence. Deliverance will certainly come in the end, St. Cuthbert reassures his audience. This argument in favor of the virtue of continued, long-term suffering is excised in

---

111 David Underdown, *Royalist Conspiracy in England 1649–1660* (New Haven: Yale Univ. Press, 1960), 247–50.

112 *Calendar, Clarendon Papers* 4:319; Underdown, 30, 34–35, 205; W. G. Hoskins, *A New Survey of England: Devon* (Newton Abbot: David & Charles, 1972), 236–38.

113 Underdown, 254–85.

Knightley's translation. Evidently, he considered it to be no longer appropriate in present circumstances. Gone too is the future-oriented note of the original. Whereas Drury's Cuthbert states that Alfred "will" be monarch of a greater kingdom in the near future ("Deo annuente, Regna maiora occupat; / Monarcha mox futurus et regni caput" [lines 3–4]), Knightley has St. Cuthbert declare in the present tense, "Now Heau'n doth reinthrone him, and, you see / Invests with great Britaine's Monarchy" (lines 3–4). This translation, along with the suppression of the second part of the epilogue, shifts the emphasis to point with anticipation to Charles's imminent re-enthronement, even while acknowledging (as the original does) that England remains "from ye worlds true faith ... kept apart" (line 10).

Given this evidence, it appears that the translation of *Aluredus* was *completed* as late as March 1660. However, the project was probably *begun* in the early winter of 1659, when royalist prospects were bleaker. Hence a composition date for *Alfrede* of 1659–1660.

Sources

The subject of Drury's tragicomedy, King Alfred's loss of his throne and his subsequent reinstatement, is historically based. To this matter the playwright added a non-historical farcical action and a melodramatic romantic strand that includes an assault upon the virtue of Alfred's eldest daughter. For his historical material Drury drew from Latin texts and Raphael Holinshed's *The Historie of England* (1587).[114] Although Edgar Hall contends that Drury went to Holinshed "for the greater portion of the historical groundwork of his play, that portion which does not come from the legends of the two saints, Cuthbert and Neot," [115] it can be shown that Drury relied as much or more on his religious-historical sources for that "groundwork."

Considering that Drury was a professor and priest, his knowledge of the Latin hagiographical sources pertaining to Alfred is unremarkable. In fact, Drury was able to fill out Holinshed's account of Alfred's reign in just those places where the Protestant chronicler fails to report hagiographical matter pertaining to Alfred's relationship with St. Cuthbert and St. Neot.

The original source for the histories of Alfred's reign was *The Life of King Alfred* by Asser, bishop of Sherborne (ca. 900), a work available in Bishop Matthew Parker's famous Latin edition with Anglo-Saxon char-

---

[114] Hall, 26–31.

[115] Hall, 26.

acters, *Alfredi Regis res gestae* (1574). A second edition by Ben Jonson's schoolmaster, William, Camden entitled *Anglica, Normannica, Hibernica, Cambrica, a veteribus scripta ex quibus Asser Meneuensis* (1602; 2nd edn, 1603) is a virtual reproduction of Parker's. As the oldest source on Alfred, Asser's chronologically organized biography permits us to fix the period in which Drury's tragicomedy is set: the winter and spring of 878–879. During this period the Viking army under Gothrum successfully routed Alfred at his royal estate at Chippenham in Wiltshire, forcing the Anglo-Saxons to flee overseas or to submit to the Danes. This low point in Alfred's military career became the focus of a set of fabled tales upon which Drury drew.

There is, however, strong reason to believe that Drury had recourse not just to Asser, whose account of Alfred's career is relatively brief, and not merely to Holinshed, but also to the more embellished versions of Alfred's life produced by two twelfth-century scribes who incorporated materials found in neither Asser nor Holinshed. The first and most important of these scribes was the monk Simeon of Durham, who introduced important new material to Asser's text, including the story of Alfred's meeting with the disguised St. Cuthbert. Although Simeon's work was not printed until 1652 (when Roger Twysden's *Historia Anglicanae scriptores* appeared), it was available in many manuscripts; even Holinshed cites him as an authority.[116] In addition to Simeon's *Historia regum*, which contains yearly chronicles of Alfred's reign, the *Historia Dunelmensis ecclesiae*, the *Historia de Sancto Cuthberto*, and the *De miraculis et translationibus Cuthberti* contain essential materials on Cuthbert's special relationship to Alfred not found in Parker's edition of Asser. [117]

The second scribe on whose work Drury drew was William of Malmesbury, whose *De gestis regum Anglorum* Sir Henry Savile edited in 1596.[118] It contains a distinctive variation, upon which Drury relies, on St. Cuthbert's appearance before Alfred in a dream.

Complicating our understanding of Drury's use of these sources is the fact that Holinshed himself, compiler that he was, drew upon the

---

[116] Simeon of Durham, *Symeonis Monachi Opera omnia*, 2 vols., ed. Thomas Arnold (London, 1857; repr. London: Kraus, 1965), 1:xv–xix; Raphael Holinshed, *The Historie of England from the time it was first inhabited vntil the time it was last conquered* (London, 1587), 146–50.

[117] See Arnold, 1:204–5; 229–33. Quotations and page numbers from Simeon's works, including *Historia regum, Historia Dunelmensis ecclesiae, Historia de Sancto Cuthberto*, and *De miraculis et translationibus Cuthberti*, are from Arnold's edition.

[118] The standard Latin edition of William's works, which I cite from, here and elsewhere, is *Willelmi Malmesbiriensis Monachi Gesta regum Anglorum, atque historia novella*, 2 vols., ed. Thomas D. Hardy (London: English Historical Society, 1840; Vaduz: Kraus Reprints, 1964).

same scholarly Latin sources to which Drury had independent access. To distinguish between these two kinds of sources, it is important to determine what matter Holinshed reports and what he omits. With respect to St. Cuthbert, for example, Holinshed preserves just one tale. It describes how the saint appeared to the slumbering Alfred,

> declaring to him, that within a while fortune should so turne, that he should recouer againe his kingdome to the confusion of his enimies. And to assure him that this should proue true, he told him that his men which were gone abroad to catch fish, should bring home great plentie, although the season was against them, by reason that the waters were frozen and that a cold rime fell that morning, to the hinderance of their purpose.[119]

The most striking feature of Holinshed's version is that it steers away from the hagiographical aspects of St. Cuthbert's epiphany. There is good reason for this. As a sixteenth-century Protestant chronicler, Holinshed places little emphasis on the miraculous powers attributed to the saint—in fact, the words "miracle" and "miraculous" are nowhere to be found in the passage. Instead, he highlights the dream or premonition of Alfred's success in regaining his kingdom, a point that dovetails nicely with the nationalistic ideology of his chronicles of England.

By contrast, Drury unstintingly follows the hagiographical reportage of his pre-Reformation sources. Most notably, he introduces a major figure totally absent from Holinshed, St. Neot, the hermit of Cornwall. Drury inventively dramatizes the legendary healing powers of this anchorite by showing Neotus bringing the lifeless Gormo and Osberne back to life and then effecting their conversion. Further, Drury has Neotus provide a refuge for Alfred's beleaguered daughters, Edelvitha and Elgina. Drawing upon the legend that St. Neot became the king's spiritual mentor and confessor, Drury also shows how Neotus brought Alfred to a Christian-stoic acceptance of his afflictions, and acknowledgment of "ye errours of [his] life / . . . / . . . and [his] owne wickednesse" (4.2.96–98).[120]

The celebrated tale of Alfred and the cakes also originates in these hagiographical sources. First recorded in the *Vita S. Neoti,* the story had been repeatedly elaborated by the time Drury received it. The es-

119 Holinshed, Raphael, *The Historie of England from the time it was first inhabited vntil the time it was last conquered* (London, 1587), 146.

120 On these matters see the editorial comments of Simon Keynes and Michael Lapidge in *Alfred the Great: Asser's Life of King Alfred and other Contemporary Sources,* trans. Simon Keynes and Michael Lapidge (Harmondsworth: Penguin, 1983), 254–55, 197–202; also Hall, 35–36.

sence of the fable, transmitted in several versions, is simple enough: Following his flight from the Danes, the disguised Alfred found refuge in a swineherd's cottage. The swineherd's wife, by tradition a virago, instructed Alfred to watch over some cakes she was baking. When the preoccupied Alfred forgot to do so and the cakes burned, the wife, not knowing to whom she spoke, scolded the king. Alfred's refusal to punish the woman and his humble acceptance of her rebuke provided Christian apologists with ample opportunity to expound upon the king's virtues. Without actually dramatizing the story of the cakes, Drury reproduced the setting of this folk tale, showing the disguised Alfred living in the cottage of the swineherd and, as later versions emphasized, in proximity to his shrewish wife.[121] The particular version that Drury dramatized may be found in Simeon's *Historia de Sancto Cuthberto* and the *De miraculis*.[122]

Drury also adopts Simeon's hostile attitude toward the Danes for their wanton cruelty and barbarism. The *De miraculis* commences by offering a lengthy account of their atrocities during Alfred's reign, a taste of which is conveyed in the sentence, "Videres tunc virgines rapi, matronalia, jura solvi, infantes ab ipsis matrum uberibus avulsos, ad terram alios elidi, per pedes alios suspendi, inter manus barbarorum alios discerpi."[123] The harsh extravagance of this account, which may be roughly translated as, "then you would see virgins raped, marriage ordinances broken, infants torn away from their mothers' breasts, some dashed to the ground, some hanged by their feet, some destroyed at the hands of barbarians," is the kind Drury himself employs in the opening scene of *Aluredus* when he has Athelrede describe the "purpl'ed" rivers, and the "great flouds of blood, drunk with ye current / wch flowes from wonded, slaughterd Carcases" (5–7). By contrast, Holinshed's presentation of the Danish conquest is relatively unemotional and businesslike.

The case Edgar Hall makes for the priority of Holinshed proves, in

---

[121] See the commentary of Keynes and Lapidge, 197–202. In his *Alfredi Regis res gestae*, Matthew Parker (London, 1574), followed by William Camden in his *Anglica, Normannica, Hibernica, Cambrica, a veteribus scripta ex quibus Asser Meneuensis* (Frankfurt, 1602; 2nd ed., 1603), interpolated the cakes tale into his translation, believing that his source, the *Annals of St. Neots*, had been composed by Asser himself.

[122] *Historia de Sancto Cuthberto* and *De miraculis* 1:204, 230–31.

[123] *De miraculis* 1:230.

fact, to be considerably overstated.[124] This is especially apparent with respect to issues of specific indebtedness. For example, Hall asserts that the three Danish kings, whom Drury names "Halfdenus, Hinguar, Hubba" (3.13.1), "were no doubt suggested by Holinshed's three; their names are however in no case the same or similar, but were taken from elsewhere in Holinshed, or from sources outside Holinshed."[125] As it turns out, Simeon is Drury's source. These names all appear the *Historia regum* under the year 866 in the same section that introduces the character of Alfred and in the same order as Drury presents them.[126] Similarly, Drury's apparition episode, in which St. Cuthbert presents himself to the sleeping Alfred, can be shown to derive from Simeon. In Knightley's translation, St. Cuthbert's message is that two tokens will provide Alfrede with "an assured marke" of his future triumph: "y^{r} Landlord shall returne / loaded with a great quantity of fish, / And y^{r} soldiers impale [i.e., surround] you with their troopes" (4.10.14–17). Only Simeon, not Holinshed, makes the arrival of new soldiers—"quingenti ad te convenient, omnes bene armati"—a token of Alfred's future conquest.[127]

William of Malmesbury must be reckoned as an important, but limited, hagiographical source for *Aluredus*. William devotes little space in the *Gesta regum Anglorum* to Alfred's life as a fugitive from the Danes, makes no mention of the swineherds, and offers almost no details about Alfred's family. Yet, it is William who incorporates the variation of the miracle of the fish catch that Drury followed in portraying St. Cuthbert's appearance before Alfred in a dream.[128] A second anecdote found in neither Simeon nor Holinshed assures us of Drury's reliance upon William. In it the king, disguised as a minstrel, enters the Danish camp and gathers the intelligence necessary to defeat his foes.[129] Drury's decision to represent all these tokens of Alfred's success indicates that the author's strategy was to synthesize his religious-historical materials on Alfred.

---

124 Hall (29), focusing on William of Malmesbury as Holinshed's primary source, mentions Simeon merely as a source for William, lumping Simeon's work unexamined with that of the other northern chroniclers, Florence of Worcester and Henry of Huntington.

125 Hall, 31.

126 *Historia regum* 2:104.

127 *De miraculis* 1:233; repeated in *Historia Cuthberto* 1:205; *Historia Dunelmensis ecclesiae* 1:62–63.

128 *Gesta regum Anglorum* 1:180–81. Holinshed also relied on William's account but reduced the two tokens to Alfred's success, observing that the fishermen returned "with so great foison of fish, that the same *might haue supplied* a great armie of men for the vittelling of them at that season" (146; emphasis mine).

129 *Gesta regum Anglorum* 1:181.

These examples illustrate the inadvisability of attempting to distinguish too sharply between Drury's "historical" and "hagiographical" sources. With respect to the materials on the Danish conquest, Simeon appears to be Drury's source, just as William appears to be his source for the report of Alfred's surveillance of his enemies. Virtually all of the miraculous matter in *Aluredus* is taken from Drury's Latin sources rather than from the derivative, incomplete account offered by Holinshed.

In view of these findings, a question arises as to how much Holinshed's chronicles really influenced Drury. Despite Hall's over-emphasis on the importance of Holinshed as the source for *Aluredus*, his claim is at bottom sound and illuminating. Particularly helpful is Hall's finding that the forms of numerous names appearing in Drury's list of dramatis personae derive from Holinshed. For example, whereas Simeon gives Alfred's mother's name as "Osburg,"[130] Drury, like Holinshed, employs the form "Osburga." In most cases Drury employs forms that are the same as, or closer to, those in Holinshed than those in William or Simeon.[131]

Proof of the soundness of Hall's discovery is the fact that it can be corroborated on other grounds. Tellingly, the historical figure Gormo, appearing under this name in Drury's play, and as "Gurmo" in Holinshed's account of Alfred's reign,[132] is absent in Asser, Simeon, and William. Finally, it may be observed that the idea for Drury's title, *Aluredus sive Alfredus*, may have been drawn from Holinshed, since, in the marginalia introducing the reign of the great king, the chronicler writes, "*Alured or Alfred*."[133]

A prudent response to the question of Drury's use of Holinshed, then, would be that the playwright did have recourse to this English-language text. Holinshed, who lists William of Malmesbury and Simeon of Durham as sources in *his* account of Alfred's reign, may even have been Drury's most immediate source, the spark for the historical reading that informs *Aluredus sive Alfredus*. But to claim more, to claim the priority of Holinshed over the Latin sources, and especially over Simeon, is to overstate the evidence. Drury's *Aluredus* is a pietistic, nationalistic play infused with hagiographical lore. The primary matter and the world view of this play came, fittingly, from Drury's monkish sources.

For the non-historical matter in *Aluredus*, Drury assuredly drew upon his knowledge of England's professional drama. Specifically, he

---

[130] *Historia regum* 2:69.

[131] Hall, 28–30.

[132] Holinshed, 147.

[133] Holinshed, 145.

drew from dramatic motifs appearing in the apocryphal Shakespeare play *The Tragedy of Locrine* (ca. 1591). That a Jacobean playwright such as Drury should have had recourse to this early, undistinguished Elizabethan play is surprising. Published in 1595, *Locrine* was not reprinted until 1664, and no record exists of its ever having been revived.[134] Nevertheless, Drury was drawn to the tragedy, probably because of its Anglo-Saxon setting. In any event, Hall, the first to identify this source, pointed out a number of parallels linking the play to *Aluredus*.[135] At least two of these prove the case beyond reasonable doubt.

Drury's most certain borrowing from *Locrine* is the name and dramatic function of Strumbo. This unusual name does not occur in any of the historical-religious narratives pertaining to Alfred, while in both *Locrine* and *Aluredus* Strumbo appears as a low-life comic figure played. A major distinction between the two is that the Strumbo of *Locrine* is a cobbler, suitor, and hen-pecked husband, while Drury's is an adolescent. Drury also borrows at least one specific dramatic motif from *Locrine*: at the moment when the bloodied King Humber appeals to the "great commander of the starry sky" to "Rain down some food" and give him meat (4.2),[136] he suddenly discovers Strumbo, whom he mistakes for Jupiter's minister Mercury. The startled Strumbo, who indeed has meat in his pocket, can only confess, "ye are deceived. I am not Mercury; I am Strumbo." As Hall says, this scene is adapted by Drury with "genuine comic power,"[137] when the famished Alfred makes a poor table with a beggar, the disguised St. Cuthbert, while Strumbo looks on disconsolately from the hollow of a tree. Declaring his hunger satisfied, the beggar leaves, announcing mysteriously, as Knightley translates it, that "this tree will instruct you farther" (2.6.32–33). When Alfred subsequently addresses the tree, Strumbo stupidly responds, "I am an Oracle, but certainly foretelling my owne death" (lines 50–51). The device of making the clown an unintended provider of food and at the same time picturing him as a would-be providential figure works especially well in Drury's adaptation as a counterpoint to the serious theme of Alfred's unstinting charity.

A second important borrowing from *Locrine* appears in the melodramatic action in which Alfrede's queen and younger daughter are cap-

---

[134] The composition and publication dates cited in the paragraph are from E. K. Chambers, *The Elizabethan Stage*, 4 vols. (Oxford: Clarendon Press, 1923), 4:26–27.

[135] Hall, 46–55.

[136] William Kozlenko's edition of *The Tragedy of Locrine* in *Disputed Plays of William Shakespeare* (New York: Hawthorn Books, 1974) is not lineated.

[137] Hall, 50.

tured by Rollo and threatened with concubinage and rape. The parallel to *Locrine* occurs when Estrild, wife of the slain King Humber, is captured by enemy soldiers and, like Osburga, is offered to King Locrine as booty. Locrine's offer of concubinage to Estrild is followed by a lengthy passage (as in *Aluredus*) in which the two adversaries debate their respective positions in sententious stichomythic exchanges. Although the two plots subsequently diverge (Estrild yields to Locrine; Osburga resolutely holds out against Rollo), the similarity in the situations of the two captured queens and their moral dilemma, all sententiously treated in the Senecan manner, is good evidence of influence.[138] Drury's use of this melodramatic material as well as of Strumbo as a comic figure in *Aluredus* provides convincing evidence that *Locrine* was a dramatic source for his mixed-mode tragicomedy.

Seneca, too, although not a source, is a pervasive influence on *Aluredus*. Seneca provided Drury with a fund of forensic philosophical material on fortune, patience, despair, lust, ambition, and the duties of kings, all of which appear in Knightley's translation of *Aluredus*.[139] Stylistically, Seneca provided the impetus for the distilled expression of wisdom and feeling in the forms of *sententiae*, stichomythia, and self-analyzing soliloquy in which the speaker is torn between opposing choices.

Even in its English incarnation, Drury's play is heavily Senecan. Its predilection for dramatizing extreme states of feeling, especially apprehension, is characteristic of both university drama and Senecan tragedy on the popular stage. The tendency in the serious scenes toward sustained rhetorical displays of grandiloquence, however, is characteristic of academic drama.[140] Still, it is important to keep in mind that

---

[138] Hall's other claims, including his belief that Drury is indebted to Peele's *The Old Wives' Tale*, Fletcher's *The Mad Lover*, and Shakespeare's *The Winter's Tale* (the latter because Autolycus picks a wallet out of the Clown's pocket) (55–62), all fail to establish clear and persuasive connections to a unique source.

[139] On the extent of this influence in seventeenth-century drama, see G. M. Ross, "Seneca's Philosophical Influence," in *Seneca*, ed. C. D. N. Costa (London and Boston: Routledge & Kegan Paul, 1974), 116–65; and H. W. Wells, "Senecan Influence on Elizabethian Tragedy: A Re-Estimation," *Shakespeare Association Bulletin* 19 (1944): 71–84.

[140] The staple studies of university drama are by Frederick Samuel Boas *University Drama in the Tudor Age* (Oxford: Oxford Univ. Press, 1914) and George Charles Moore Smith, *College Plays Performed in the University of Cambridge* (Cambridge: Cambridge Univ. Press, 1923). Treatments of Seneca on the professional stage usually begin with the earlier studies by John W. Cunliffe, *The Influence of Seneca on Elizabethan Tragedy* (London: Macmillan, 1893; repr., New York: G. E. Stechert, 1907); F. L. Lucas, *Seneca and Elizabethan Tragedy* (Cambridge: Cambridge Univ. Press, 1922), Clarence Mendall, *Our Seneca* (New Haven: Yale Univ. Press, 1941), and H. B. Charlton, *The Senecan Tradition in Renaissance Tragedy* (Manchester: Univ. of Manchester Press, 1946). Important reassessments of the tradition may be

Seneca's influence on academic and professional drama both was pervasive. The strands of influence cannot always be separated. For example, Jasper Heywood (1535–1598)—whose mother was related to Sir Thomas More and whose sister was John Donne's mother—was a leader of the English Jesuit mission in 1581 and (previously) a professor at the Jesuit University of Dillingen in Bavaria.[141] His pioneering translations were responsible for bringing Seneca into prominence on the Elizabethan stage. By the time that the English-raised Drury was writing *Aluredus,* plays composed in the Senecan manner had become legion on both academic and professional stages.

A reader who did not know that Knightley's *Alfrede* is a translation of *Aluredus* might well believe that several passages are translations taken from Seneca's own plays. The passages in which Elfrede wanders "in the vmbrage of a wood" and "A horrour lodg'd ith' trees excited feare / wch mou'ed by the wind made a dolefull noise" (2.1.32–34) and in which Gothurnus, beholding the "ghosts" of Osberne and Gormo, recoils (in the manner of Thyestes or Oedipus)—"What suddain Horrour seases on my ioynts, / and benums my hand? I tremble with chilnesse / and Amazement" (5.14.104–6)—are as fine examples as may be found of Senecan pathetic fallacy and the physiological effects of horror. It is probably too much to claim, as Hall does, that Drury "seems to have avoided carefully even the close verbal echo of the Roman,"[142] yet Drury's *Aluredus* does indeed avoid quoting Seneca's verses directly.

This fact suggests that Seneca is the opposite of a major source; he is a major influence, a model for the kind of imitation in which one elaborates, reconfigures, and imaginatively re-presents the master.

Critical Interpretation

I

Despite a theatrical heritage that had previously treated virtually every reign of note in English history, Drury's *Aluredus sive Alfredus* is

---

found in Jean Jacquot, ed., *Les Tragèdies de Senèque et le Théâtre de la Renaissance* (Paris: Centre national de la recherche scientifique, 1964), in G. K. Hunter's two essays—"Seneca and the Elizabethans: a Case Study in 'Influence,'" *Shakespeare Survey* 20 (1967): 17–26, and "Seneca and English Tragedy," in *Seneca,* 166–204—and in A. L. Motto and John R. Clark's "Senecan Tragedy: a Critique of Scholarly Trends," *Renaissance Drama* 6 (1973): 219–35.

[141] *DNB,* s.v. "Heywood, Jasper."

[142] Hall, 40.

the first dramatic treatment of King Alfred's reign, and Robert Knightley's translation the first English dramatization of his reign. The subject was not treated again until 1778, when John Home made *Alfred, A Tragedy*, a thoroughly romanticized melodrama with Mrs. Barry as Alfred's betrothed.[143]

Two consequences of *Alfrede or Right Reinthron'd* having remained in manuscript are that it is virtually unknown to scholars and that its close relationship to *Aluredus sive Alfredus* was unrecognized until quite recently.[144] References to *Alfrede* are rare. Harbage mentions it approvingly in *Cavalier Drama* as a play that "returns to an older, fresher day," and Lois Potter, describing it as "extremely enjoyable," treats it as an example of the banished-ruler play in a pastoral setting.[145]

Categorizing it as a banished-ruler play places *Alfrede* within a significant dramatic tradition. Readers wishing to know more about this may consult Potter's study. There is, however, another significant, unaddressed question pertaining to material culture that *Alfrede* and the original *Aluredus* raise. How could the same play, albeit written first in Latin and then in Engish, function as a topical religious-political drama, as it did, for two different generations of Catholic readers (separated by forty years)? To raise the issue is to ask how plays, functioning diachronically within culture, can come to convey a plurity of significances.

Post-structuralist theory has taught us that meaning does not reside sovereignly within texts but in interpretive communities, whose limited corporate authority creates no single fixed meaning but rather indeterminate, contingent meanings that shift with time.[146] The case of the devolution of *Aluredus* offers an instructive illustration of how shifting social-political contexts, then as now, forge new topical significances.

Drury's *Aluredus* was initially created in 1619 as a homiletic drama for English Catholic audiences. In retelling, but nevertheless subordi-

---

[143] John Home, *Alfred, a Tragedy* (London, 1778), in *The Plays of John Home*, ed. James S. Malek (New York and London: Garland, 1980), list of *Dramatis Personae.*

[144] Lois Potter, *Secret Rites and Secret Writing: Royalist Literature, 1641–1660* (Cambridge: Cambridge Univ. Press, 1989), 106. As stated in the Acknowledgements, I am deeply obliged to Professor Potter, who apprized me of this crucial fact prior to the publication of her book.

[145] Alfred Harbage, *Cavalier Drama* (New York: Modern Language Association, 1936, repr. New York: Russell & Russell, 1964), 235; Potter, *Secret Rites*, 106.

[146] See, for example, Louis Montrose, "Professing the Renaissance: The Poetics and Politics of Culture," in *The New Historicism*, ed. H. Aram Veeser (New York and London: Routledge, 1989), 23; Roland Barthes, "From Work to Text," *Textual Strategies: Perspectives in Post-Structuralist Criticism*, ed. Josué Harari (Ithaca: Cornell Univ. Press, 1979), 73–81.

nating history to moral philosophy—as most serious Renaissance dramatists did—Drury worked to reinforce Catholic precepts of conduct and faith. His play can also be seen to function in a topical ideological context, addressing the social-political question of how Catholics should face the reality of their religion's displacement in England. When Robert Knightley undertook to translate the play in 1659, it still retained its doctrinal significance; but by virtue of its new political context, it acquired a series of altered topical meanings.

The most stable of these inheres in the play's Christian code of conduct and Catholic world view. The crucial problems Drury confronts—not as sovereign author, but as a prominent speaker addressing a communal concern—are how England, a heretical nation, is to be returned to the fold, and how in the interim its displaced faithful might endure. The underlying difficulties inherent in the play's articulating both a stoic doctrine of indifference to the world (fortune) and an active involvement in England's religious-political fate are not easily reconciled. These may best be approached by examining the play's own exploration of mutability and of the most appropriate defense against its effects.

The idea of mutability encompasses three related beliefs in Drury's tragicomedy: first, the natural tendency of all things, due to the effects of the Fall, is to degenerate (modern entropy). Second, political institutions such as monarchy are under constant attack from social forces that would destroy their order-preserving principles, leading countries ever closer to the chaos toward which they naturally tend. Third, a divine providence, which has punished England for its sins, nevertheless oversees its welfare. This belief system, in which history is read doctrinally as a decline from an original state of perfection, underlies so much of seventeenth-century thought that it even informs texts that do not explicitly invoke it.

Nevertheless, Knightley's translation of Drury's Prologue makes explicit the effects of mutability. Without "the divine P[r]otection," St. Cuthbert explains, "How short, vnconstant, is ye life Men liue" (lines 20–21). In the absence of divine intervention "Obtained by the sacred prayres of Saints" (line 22), it would be true that "Mortall things without a Rule are hurl'd" (line 5). So too, as St. Cuthbert declares in the Epilogue, England has become "ffrom Heau'n rebelliously degenerate" (line 12) because it has, in the literal sense, fallen away from its ancestral birthright. England's entire encounter with the Danes—and, by analogy, with the revolutionary forces released by Parliament and its model armies during the Commonwealth and Protectorate—is an encounter with barbarism, which, as the Prologue informs us, breaks ratified peace treaties, defiles ancient "holy Alters" (line 13), and overthrows settled kingdoms.

To create a sense of the wanton destruction wrought by the degenerate armies of Gothurnus, Drury repeatedly evokes the primal images of fire and flood. The affective power of such images is particularly apparent in Knightley's rendering of the passage in which Athelrede laments that the insulting Danes overrun all, making the earth

> weepe great flouds of blood, drunk with ye current
> wch flowes from wonded, slaughterd Carcases:
> Rivers are purpl'ed, and roughly glide along
> Their reedy banks hasting to the Ocêan. (1.1.5–8)

The sense of excess is apparent. Other features are more subtle. The image of blood flowing into the sea suggests the effacement of English identity. Purpled English blood is becoming mixed with water and dissolved in the common sea. This apprehension of effacement—of the obliteration of one's family honor and name, nation, way of life, and ancient religion—is the most compelling anxiety in the play.

"Change," understood as meaning "degenerate change," is the palpable reality the play's principal characters confront. For the tragicomedy's pious Christians, the insistent dramatic question becomes how they can endure the collapse of their world. Temptations to commit suicide are everywhere. For Alfrede above all the persisting issue is how a dethroned king constrained to discard his regal robes and scepter can avoid falling into despair. This trauma proceeds from the acute anxiety that Providence may be unconcerned about the fate of the established Tudor-Stuart social and political order. For this basic reason, the type of dilemma Alfrede faces has been recurringly represented in other English histories, including *King Lear, Richard II* and Marlowe's *Edward II*.

Although disheartened and famished, Alfred undergoes a test of charity put to him by St. Cuthbert, and then the harder test of dignified acceptance of self in misfortune put to him by Neotus. The reward for attaining a state of indifference to worldly goods and glory and an equanimous self-acceptance is God's indulgent "Mercy," which "promises far / greater Kingdoms then those ye Dane possesse" (4.2.130–31). Modern readers may take notice that this quietism is problematic in that it contradicts the play's religious-political goal, explicitly articulated in the epilogue, of reconverting England to Catholicism. This pervasive philosophical tension is evident even in the subtitle with which Knightley dubs his translation. The question pointedly arises as to whether Catholics are to promote or not to promote the agenda of "right" being "reinthron'd." Doctrinally, the only escape from this latent contradiction is an appeal to the workings of Providence and a willingness to submit oneself to the divine wisdom that resolves all.

With respect to Catholic dogma, *Aluredus* is interesting for its humanistic attempt to reconcile paganism and Christianity on the issue of suicide. Whereas the pagan stoics (most notably Cato), Rome's military heroes, Brutus and Antony, and such Christian humanists as George Chapman in *The Revenge of Bussy D'Ambois* embraced the doctrine that a person's life was his own to dispose of when the rude world offered no relief, Drury promulgates a Roman Catholic brand of stoicism that explicitly rejects suicide as a solution to life's problems. Along with Alfrede, several other displaced characters, including Alfrede's mother and his sister Elgine, also face this temptation and learn to carry on. As they wander through the marshes and woods of Athelnea in their exile, all eventually find refuge in the modest cottage of Denevulphe or in the rural hermitage of Neotus, who instructs them in the virtues of Christian suffrance.

This spectacle of royalty put out of office and discovering in its humiliation life's core values follows a pattern analogous to that of *King Lear,* in which the hovel and the heath become the strange turf where loyal retainers reaffirm by acts of fidelity their entitlement to their original places in a restored social order. This homology says less about the greatness of Drury's play than about the persistence of a form of dramatic representation that reinscribes the rightness of the status quo ante. The prospect of Elgine's rape and the Queen's forced concubinage to the Danish king functions toward a similar end. These are not merely melodramatic motifs; the threats to the selfhood and bodily integrity of Alfrede's female relatives also function ideologically to parallel the threat of England's becoming "adulterated" (in the root sense) by the rape and miscegenation of the royal family. At the same time, Elgine's and Edelvitha's exemplary behavior under these stresses works to demonstrate their entitlement to the royal status of which they have been deprived.

At this level, the contradiction inherent in promoting both a personal ethics of indifference to fortune and an engaged political ideology is effaced by the play's celebration of the re-establishment of England's royalty and faithful nobility. In this harmonious outcome rank—translated as temporal power—is perfectly restored (in the romanticized, fundamentally royalist, tragicomic mode) in accord with the spiritual status attained by each character. From this vantage, the seeming quiltwork of discrete motifs and interesting character types in *Aluredus* is revealed to be the surface manifestation of a single ideological conception: the calculus from which all assessments issue is the humanist one of self-realization, interpreted narrowly in terms of spiritual development. The play is thus focused on psychological states, which are the key to the assessment of character and social worth.

From this perspective, Gothurnus is not merely a ludicrous, ranting Herod; he is the primary vehicle for dramatizing the failure to cultivate (Christian) patience and self-control, and his rule is shown to be unkingly because he cannot negotiate the world's mutability. Unable to govern himself, he cannot credibly govern others. Alternatively put, Gothurnus is not, in humanist terms, an autonomous individual; he is a play-king precisely because he is "subjected" by his emotions (Drury recognizes no other limitation, institutional or historical, upon the individual's freedom to choose). This failure of Gothurnus's is epitomized with Senecan pithiness when Alfrede says, "How impatiently an insolent Tyrant endures adversity" (5.2.9).

The pattern evident in the contrasting pairing of Alfrede with Gothurnus also manifests itself in other pairings and in thescenes of stichomythic riposte. Both work to highlight the moral discipline necessary to resist the effects of mutability. Even in the comic subplot, Drury develops this theme, depicting Titmus's struggle to maintain his personal honor in the face of his terrorizing rival, Bragadocia. Employing the master idiom of the play, Titmus resolves to teach his oppressor that he, Titmus, "doe[s] not degenerate from ye noble Progeny of Pigmies" (5.2.32). By the play's end, the blustery Bragadocia is bridled and then ridden by his betters. This bridling of Bragadocia is allegorically significant and owes something to the Elizabethan interlude for *The Trial of Treasure* (1567) and the actors in *Sir Thomas More* (c. 1593–c. 1601). Each introduces a character called Inclination, whose incontinence and braggadocio are subdued by his being bridled and ridden. Following this manner of dramaturgy, Drury employs the little people of his comic imagination—alongside the great ones—to uphold a primeval order of virtue.

The wisdom of bridling the passions in order to inure oneself to the vicissitudes of fortune is a recurring homiletic theme. Whereas Titmus and Bragodocia dramatize the doctrine, Neotus verbalizes it with somber flair:

He's free alone from feare
and triumphs ore ye world that liues vnmou'd
and vnconcern'd at ye change of fortune;
who knows how to bridle his desires,
and regulate ye passions of his Minde;
who leauing earthly for eternall Goods,
hoards vp an vncreased Treasure. (4.18.31–37)

Many of the serious scenes dramatize this stoic-Christian wisdom with stylized self-consciousness. Both the characters themselves and the folly or wisdom they express are set forth in memorable counterpoint. When, for example, the Danish officer Rollo encourages Edelvitha to contemplate her people's ruin and her daughter's rape (4.17), the queen responds with an oration on the quality of mercy; and when this fails she fends off each of Rollo's arguments with a stichomythic repartee (lines 97–110). A variation on this pattern occurs when the self-seeking materialist Gormo threatens Humfrey (1.10) in the first hemistiche of each line from 17 to 39, and Humfrey systematically inverts every thrust with catechismic expressions of stoic-Christian patience and faith in the second hemistiche. Similar passages pit Gothurnus against the newly converted Osberne on the subject of love and grief (5.5.40–52) and, later, in repartees built on a two-line structure, on the theme of self-control as true kingship (5.14.5–23). These passages, in turn, dovetail with the earlier didactic scenes (3.9.; 4.2.; 4.18) in which Neotus converts Osberne and Gormo to Christianity and instructs Alfrede in Christian self-control. All are carefully crafted, virtuoso passages that provide religious instruction within the tragicomic pattern of the reconciliation and reinstallation of the Christian characters.

From a post-structuralist perspective, we may observe that the outstanding feature of these recurring debates is in fact an absence, the absence, to be precise, of a credible ideology that can stand in opposition to the play's Catholic theology. Gothurnus comes across as a ranting fool not only because he is an emotional misfit, but also because he is not given a meaningful political world view. Pagan that he is, Gothurnus is made to affirm a ludicrous version of "natural" self-interest characterized by unrestrained emotional displays. In the logic of the play, Gothurnus is simply a victim of uncontrolled "ambition" or "will." This presentation of the villain strictly in terms of his psychology, which is then theatricalized by unrestrained emotional displays, defines the only reality he is permitted to inhabit, and determines the sole explanation for his cruelty. For all his strutting and fretting, Gothurnus is truly "spoken for"; he is ventriloquized into a bombastic nothingness, a booming silence.

II

From a topical standpoint the real doctrinal or political debate in which Drury engages is an intra-Catholic one. As Edgar Hall argues, when Drury presented *Aluredus* at Douai in 1619, he was addressing a bitter contemporary controversy between the Jesuits and the Benedictines regarding the means by which England should be reconverted to Catholicism.[147] Whereas the Jesuits championed active resistance and subversion, the Benedictines and lay clerics, including Drury, favored pacific means.[148] Such a reading may be disputed on the general grounds that Drury was educated by the politically activist

---

[147] Hall, 22–26.

[148] Dures, 67–69.

Jesuits,[149] or that his play frequently shows Alfred's retainers engaging in combat. Nevertheless, Hall's reconstruction finds much support in the play. For one thing, Drury shapes his historical materials to make Alfred's spiritual recovery dependent upon the pacifistic instruction of St. Neot. For another, Drury's epilogue, which gives the playwright an opportunity to speak from a position outside of the action of the play, explicitly exalts patience over brutish warfare. There Drury has St. Cuthbert appeal to his audience to eschew arms such as giants bear and to grasp instead the weapons of Christian piety and faith, conquering by enduring ("non illa horrido / Devota Marti, qualia gigantes gerunt: / Sed illa Christiana doctrinam, fidem,/ Patiendo vince" [lines 28–31]). In this way, Drury's *Aluredus* transcends its remote setting to become for its Catholic audiences of 1619 and its readership of the 1620s a timely address on the best way to repair the ravages of mutability in the early seventeenth century.

Robert Knightley's relationship to this set of significances is ambiguous. He is at once a reader of Drury's play and a maker of that play in another language. In this role Knightley shows himself to be touched by the play less as entertainment or even as historical reconstruction than as ethical paradigm. Gracefully commending *Alfrede* to his sister, Robert declares, "it can represent to your intellect not what is, but what should haue bin written" (Dedication, lines 16–18). Knightley believes in the moral efficacy of literature, which, as Sidney argued in *An Apology for Poetry* (1595), possesses the unexcelled power of being able to represent experience concretely while still "winning the mind from wickedness to virtue."[150] However, Knightley says nothing of the role of pleasure in the poet's exciting readers to virtue, insisting, rather, on the idealizing power of literature. Instead of merely presenting the particulars of history, literature can evince the broader reality behind experience, revealing its philosophic generality. For Knightley, the artistic representation of the historical particulars of Alfred's reign could effectively convey a sense of the general moral laws governing human behavior. This invocation of a prescribed moral order—the world as it ought to be—motivates the translator's inventive representation of Alfred's restoration as anticipating and in a sense guaranteeing the restoration of the Stuart monarchy.

This latter, topical purpose of Knightley's causes him to accentuate the political theology of the play he translates. When Knightley endows Drury's Alfred play with the new subtitle, *or Right Reinthron'd,*

---

[149] Siconolfi, 25–26.

[150] Philip Sidney, *An Apology for Poetry* (1595), ed. Forrest G. Robinson (Indianapolis: Bobbs-Merrill, 1970), 38.

he introduces an ideological thrust: the restoration of Alfred betokens the restoration of his latter-day typological embodiment. We might say that Knightley conveys this meaning as an author, not a translator. The reason for his doing so rests in the reading practices of seventeenth-century audiences. The analogic method of reading history and historical literature had a well-established history. Tacitus and other Roman historians, along with Machiavelli, were read for "prognostic" or "politic" analysis to determine the principles by which governments in fact worked.[151] Ben Jonson articulated this method of seeing the present in the past when he declared in his *Conversations with Drummond* that "Tacitus wrott the secrets of the [Privy] Councill and Senate, as Suetoniũs did those of the Cabinet and the Coũrte."[152] Similarly, the reading of events in "parallel" is a practice that Jonson dramatizes in *Sejanus* when he shows how Roman historians were judged seditious because their work "paralels / The times," "vpbraid[s] the age" and/or "taxe[s] the present state."[153] Incontrovertible evidence that readers themselves employed such reading strategies comes from the marginalia in Philip Herbert's edition of Chapman's *The Conspiracy and Tragedy of Charles Duke of Byron* (1608), in which events in France at the turn of the seventeenth century are read in the context of English politics in the 1630s.[154]

Corroboration that such prognostic reading is being encouraged in both *Aluredus* and *Alfrede* may be found in their prologues and epilogues. Drury never calls the kingdom over which Alfred ruled West Saxony or Wessex, and Alfred's people are not called Saxons or Anglo-Saxons (common appellations in the sources available to Drury); rather, he calls Alfred's country "Anglia" (that is, "England") or "Brittania," and his people "Britans." These broader terms are applicable to seventeenth-century England. Knightley enforces this connection even more strongly than Drury in the body of his text, and with special emphasis in rendering Cuthbert's epilogue. There Knightley has Cuthbert speak anachronistically not merely of "England" (Drury's "Anglia"), but of "great Britaine's Monarchy" (line 4). Following Drury again, Knightley moves completely outside the play to apostrophize the "wretched England" (line 7) of the present age.

---

[151] Annabel Patterson, *Censorship and Interpretation: The Conditions of Writing and Reading in Early Modern England* (Madison: Univ of Wisconsin Press, 1984), 44–112.

[152] *Conversations with Drummond*, 146–47, in Ben Jonson, *The Complete Works of Ben Jonson*, 11 vols., ed. C. H. Herford, and Percy and Evelyn Simpson (Oxford: Clarendon Press, 1925–52), 1:136.

[153] *Sejanus*, 2.1.308–311; 3.1.468; cf. 3.1.396, in *Jonson: Works* 4.

[154] Albert Tricomi, "Philip Earl of Pembroke and the Analogical Way of Reading Political Tragedy," *Journal of English and Germanic Philology* 85 (1986): 332–45.

So too in the play proper Knightley is attentive to this interplay of past and present, frequently employing the term "Britans" to describe Alfred's people. Remarkably, Knightley introduces a stage direction near the end of the play that is unmistakably anachronistic: when Gothurnus runs at Osberne and Gormo, the latter two *"pull of their periwigs"* (5.14.103; *"detractu capillorum"* in Drury's "argument" to 5.15).

As a method of historiography, the depiction of events in parallel demanded that the factual matter in the source(s) be respected. The force of the parallel, its "truth of argument" to borrow another phrase of Jonson's, depended on it.[155] Such a method continually left open the question of which passages could rightfully be applied to contemporary conditions. Of course, the entire procedure of establishing the operative parallels lay undefinitively in the hands of readers, for the playwright, having indicated by his promptings the aptness of an analogical reading, was (and is) powerless to control the process, a fact that carried a degree of protection for authors treating sensitive political matters.[156]

Modern readers recognize that there are serious limitations involved in attempting to discover a determinate, even if contingent, meaning in a historically situated text. If, however, the modest goals and limitations inherent in this epistemology be accepted, the following points may be emphasized as ones to which Knightley's mid-seventeenth-century, royalist readers of *Alfrede* would probably have responded:

> Alfrede's defeat of the seemingly invincible Gothurnus and the celebration of the re-establishment of Alfrede's kingship are the central facts informing this analogic interpretation. By this reading, Alfrede's victory over the godless, barbaric Danes is the analogic equivalent to Charles's victory over the parliamentarian forces with their seemingly invincible Model Army.
>
> Gothurnus's acceptance of the Christian faith works premonitorily. Since Gothurnus's rule is depicted as impious and bloody and since St. Cuthbert describes England as being "Shipwrackt vpon ye Rockes of Herisy," her "consecrated Temples" despoiled (Epilogue, lines 13–16), the imputation, it seems evident, is that the rebel Puritan regime has made England an outlaw nation and divorced her from God's grace. The Epilogue states bluntly that

---

[155] In "The Significance of Jonson's First Requirement for Tragedy: 'Truth of Argument,' " *Studies in Philology* 49 (1952): 195–213, J. A. Bryant explicates this concept.

[156] See Patterson, 44–119.

England remains separated from "ye worlds true faith" (line 10). The conversion of England under Charles II remained, therefore, a hoped-for but unfulfilled prospect in 1660.

Osberne's statement to Gothurnus that "Our foes are friends," that Alfrede's people don't harbor "perpetuall Hatred," and that "They overcome by Piety" (5.14.121–24) would echo—I think unmistakably for seventeenth-century Englishmen—the conditions of Charles's return so widely circulated prior to the formal publication of the Declaration of Breda in April 1660. As Clarendon's *State Papers* make clear, ambassadors were sent to England as early as September 1659, formally proposing "a general peace, and urging the restoration of the King who promised a general act of oblivion."[157] These political terms conform to the spirit of romantic tragicomedy, whose essence is reconciliation and forgiveness.

Knightley's foreshortened epilogue is the one place, we must keep in mind, where he consciously interposed himself between the original play and his own readership in 1660. By excising the passage in which Drury had directed his auditors of 1619 to conquer their country by faith and endurance, Robert Knightley left unspecified the means whereby "great Britaine's Monarchy" (line 4) was to redeem itself in 1660 from its "rebelliously degenerate" (line 12) condition. On the crucial question of how England is to be returned to the Catholic faith, Knightley is silent. What he *has* provided is a context from which an answer may emerge. For his Catholic readers of 1660 the hope for England's future fell implicitly to Alfred's analogic heir, Charles II, since "Heav'n doth reinthrone him" (line 3).

Characters: Analogues and Functions

St. Cuthbert is Alfrede's patron saint and the figure who heads the list of dramatis personae. Cuthbert's appearance is ahistorical in the sense that the saint lived in the mid-seventh century, long before King Alfred. St. Cuthbert reaffirms the divine oversight that guides England and sustains her virtuous rulers. Such an outlook, analogous to that in Shakespeare's late romances, is readily identifiable, as we have seen, with an aristocratic world view. As an actor and a presenter, St. Cuthbert stands both inside and outside the play, articulating the play's transcendental, pietistic, royalist belief system. His all-seeing perspec-

---

[157] *Calendar, Clarendon Papers* 4:361.

tive frames the war between the Anglo-Saxons and the Danes as a struggle between, in effect, culture and barbarism, stability and anarchy, Christianity and paganism, tradition and degenerate change. St. Çuthbert shares the stage with another saintly figure, Neotus, a character identical with the historical St. Neot, the ninth-century Saxon anchorite and kinsman of Alfred. Although the saint does not appear in Simeon or William of Malmesbury, Drury could have had recourse to Parker's (or Camden's) Asser in depicting him.[158]

For the names of Alfrede's family, Knightley substitutes English forms for Drury's Latinized names. The queen mother, "Osburga," becomes "Osberga"; the brothers "Edvardus" and "Adelvoldus" simply "Edward" and "Adelvold." The elder daughter is called "Elfreda" in both texts, while the younger, "Elgina," becomes "Elgine" in Knightley's. The king himself is simply called "Alfrede" rather than "Aluredus." However, Knightley follows Drury precisely in naming Alfred's wife "Edelvitha." Neither Drury nor Knightley includes the third daughter, recorded in all the sources, including Holinshed, who reports her name as "Ethelwitha."[159] It may be that Elgine, whose virginity is threatened by ruffian soldiers, is a conflation of Alfred's eldest and second-eldest daughters, the latter of whom (Aelthegifu) was renowned as a holy virgin and entered holy orders. On the other hand, virginity jeopardized is such a staple of romantic tragicomedy that no historical analogue is necessary to account for its presence in Drury's play.

Humfrey and Athelrede are, respectively, generals of the horse and foot. They appear to be Drury's creation, and their titles reflect seventeenth-century military divisions. Alfrede's elder brother, it may be noted, was christened "Athelrede." "Gothurnus" is Knightley's rendering of Alfred's great Danish adversary, "Guthrum," called "Gothrunnus" in Drury's text. Gothurnus's brother's name, "Osberne," appears in Asser, who identifies him as a great Viking earl.[160] By contrast, the name of the farcical figure "Gormo" may be found in Holinshed.[161] The name "Rollo" appears in both Simeon's *Historia Regum* and Holinshed's *Historie of England*.[162]

Other figures are stock types. Bragadocia is, obviously, the stock

[158] Parker, 14.
[159] Holinshed, 148.
[160] Keynes and Lapidge, 90.
[161] Holinshed, 147.
[162] *Historia Regum* 2:111; Holinshed, 146.

braggart soldier of Renaissance drama; he is actually called "Miles gloriosus" in *Aluredus*. "Pipero" is clearly a rustic's name; its Latin derivation means "pepper."[163] "Titmus," another rustic, is a variant spelling of "Titmouse," signifying a small, petty, insignificant person.[164] Drury uses the character and the diminutive name as a counterpoint to the large, blustering Bragadocia.

The swineherd Denevulphe, his wife Crabula, and their son Strumbo comprise a special sub-class. They are treated as humors characters, their depiction being the result of Drury's reading of the tale of the cakes. Philologically, "Denevulphe" means "Danish fox."[165] "Crabula," meaning "hornet" or "irritant," is a cross, ill-mannered person, and by extension, a shrew. The name, with overtones of an ill-bred country person, conforms to the tradition that the swineherd's wife was a scold.[166] "Strumbo," derived from "strumpo" or "strump," is a back-formation of "strumpet."[167]

Editorial Principles and Practices

The purpose of this edition is to present readers of seventeenth-century literature with a conservative transcription of Alfrede, while still maintaining readability. I have made this decision on the premise that scholars may consult this edition for reasons that extend beyond the desire for a readable text. Some may be interested in stylistic and orthographic matters, others in dramatic conventions or Christian terminology and allusiveness. No editor can anticipate the purposes readers may have in studying a text such as *Alfrede*. Thus I have attempted to preserve the original in most respects.

However, I have stopped short of offering a diplomatic transcription, which requires the preservation of deletions, careted insertions, and other intrusive, potentially confusing anomalies. Even diplomatic transcriptions are limited in their ability to replicate the original, since the printing of a manuscript transforms it into another medium. Readers who wish to study the hand of the author, the mixture of styles used in making majuscules such as "S" and "T," the paper, or the manuscript's untranscribable flourishes can do so only by examining the original or a photographic facsimile.

---

163 *The Oxford Latin Dictionary* (Oxford: Clarendon Press, 1968), s.v. "piper."
164 *OED*, s.v. "titmouse."
165 *OLD*, s.v. "vulpes."
166 *OLD*, s.v. "crabro."
167 *OED*, s.v. "strump."

In attempting to establish moderate, conservative grounds for emending the present edition, I have looked to several studies for guidance.[168] The kinds of emendation I have made appear in brackets in the body of the text and, where necessary, are explicated in brief textual notes. I have looked especially to Anthony G. Petti's *English Literary Hands from Chaucer to Dryden*, preserving, as he suggests, the original spelling, including minuscule "u" for "v" and "i" for "j" but, as Petti also urges, transcribing majuscules "I/J" uniformly as "I" and preserving "ff" (rendered "Ff" at the beginning of sentences) for "F".[169] In the body of the text I have introduced a letter or word in brackets where the scribe appears to have jumped over the letter or word, or where such intrusion removes ambiguity (e.g., "on[e] place"). At the suggestion of the publisher, I have not attempted to preserve the original lineation of the play's prose scenes and the prose dedication. Hyphenations at the end of prose lines, which appear as an "=" sign in the manuscript, are preserved; a bracket with a slash [/] has been introduced to show the break. Catchwords, which are not part of the play proper but appear regularly in the play text, have not been transcribed. However, I have noted all instances in the play proper where the catchword is lacking. To facilitate citation, line numbers have been introduced by act and scene in the outer margin at every tenth line.

Pagination follows the manuscript, which records each recto page. In the present edition these are recorded in brackets with the notation "fol." preceding the page number. Since the manuscript lacks verso page numbers, these too have been supplied in brackets (e.g., [fol. 3v]). In the manuscript, folio numbers appear *above* the textual matter in the right-hand margin; in the present edition, *all* folio notations appear at the end of the first line of the new page. Folio notations for prose scenes (which do not follow the lineations of the manuscript), appear at the end of the line when the break occurs. In these instances, the

---

[168] In considering paleographical and editing matters, I have in addition to Anthony G. Petti's *English Literary Hands from Chaucer to Dryden* (Cambridge: Harvard Univ. Press, 1977) relied upon Fredson Bowers's *Principles of Bibliographical Description* (Princeton: Princeton Univ. Press, 1949), W. W. Greg's, *English Literary Autographs, 1550–1650*, 2 vols. (Oxford: Oxford Univ. Press, 1932; repr. Nendeln, Lichtenstein: Kraus Reprints, 1968), and Samuel A. Tannenbaum's *The Handwriting of the Renaissance* (Columbia Univ. Press, 1930; repr. New York: Frederick Ungar, 1967), and have found especially useful Mary-Jo Kline's *Guide to Documentary Editing* (Baltimore and London: Johns Hopkins Univ. Press, 1987), which is principally concerned with the editing of manuscripts in its sixth chapter, "The Practical Application of Editorial Conventions" (132–51).

[169] Petti, 34–35.

precise place where the new page begins in the manuscript is indicated by a footnote that identifies the catchwords for these prose scenes. Where no note is offered, the reader may assume that the first word of the new folio page, often a speaker heading, is the catchword.

Decisions about whether to transcribe as minuscule or majuscule certain letter forms, including "long s" and "w," are matters for editorial judgment. To enable scholars to quote from the text more easily I have silently capitalized minuscules at the beginning of sentences. With the same end in mind, I have inserted bracketed punctuation marks, when such insertions help in making grammatical sense of the text. In those instances when the original punctuation has been replaced, the original mark is recorded in a note.

Except for the caret, which functions only as a placement marker in reading the manuscript, all diacritical marks are preserved in the text proper. Caret marks are duly noted, and the idiosyncratic # mark that appears at the beginning of scenes, and elsewhere, is also preserved. Apostrophes are transcribed as they appear in the manuscript, even when their placement differs from modern practice—e.g., "do'nt." So too, abbreviations and superscripts are represented in accord with the manuscript, although with two minor adjustments: the Alfrede scribe almost always writes "w^{ch}" with a period beneath them in the raised letters, but since this is awkward to render by mechanical means, I have not attempted to reproduce it. Instead readers should assume (unless otherwise noted) that "w^{ch}" is always rendered in the manuscript with a period beneath the superscript. All other superscripts have no period beneath the original unless explicitly noted. I have also made one minor concession to accord with modern superscript usage: whereas the manuscript renders the word "Saint" as "S^{t}" with a period beneath the "t," I have simply placed the period beside the raised letter: "$\text{S}^{\text{t.}}$"

The stage directions in Alfrede are more difficult to reproduce. To distinguish speaker parts from the dialogue, all such parts have been rendered with upper case lettering. In the manuscript, speaker parts at the left margin are set-off from the text proper and are neither underlined nor written in upper-case. Single-line stage directions generally are underlined in the manuscript, and multiple-line directions usually appear with the last line (only) underscored. I have not attempted to reproduce the marginal underlinings, overlinings, and left-sided brackets that accompany the scribe's stage directions, which are often crowded into the right margin over several lines. Directions are normally reproduced on a separate line in the appropriate place, except for same-line asides.

It may be helpful to point out that when several characters are named at the beginning of a scene, the manuscript accords the first speech to the first-named character without further identification. I preserve this convention in my transcription.

Annotations have been made of allusions and philological usages that may be vague or unfamiliar to readers.

Alfrede.
or
Right reinthron'd.
a
Tragicomedie.
x. x. x.

Prologue
St. Cuthbert.

Who this deny's that Heav'n a pious care
Retains for humain things; that saints apeare
Call'd to th' assistance of affaires below,
Must Cruelnesse ith' Deity allow
That mortall things without a Rule are hurl'd
And deeme those Spirits helplesse to ye world:
Piety's no Captive to the Orbs above
But oft unto afflicted lands doth move.
This makes me to forsake the glorious skyes
To visit my poore Cuntry w.th exhausted eyes
A prey to Mars, where the inhuman Dane
with sacrilegious Cruelty's doth staine
Our holy Altars; but I'm come to bring
Help to th' afflicted, mindfull of that King
Of my deare England, who zealously intent
So oft his prayres unto my eares hath sent.
If ever you have heard of Cuthberts Name
whom England nourished, now heav'n doth claime
I

4

I the same now will true examples give
How short, unconstant, is ye life men live
which always the divine Protection wants
Obtained by the sacred prayres of Saints.
King Alfrede vanquished by adverse fate
Now from the Danes seekes safety by retreate;
And he who yet nere knew but still t'orecome
Can from his foes scarce refuge find at home.
Thus heav'n to th' Britans punishment doth send,
Till taught by evills they their lives amend.
Loe one of th' Kings chiefe Captains doth apeare,
I goe; strait to return an Actor here.
Beginnings clad in sorrows Livery
will end in joy, content, alacrity.

Act: i. Scen: i.
Athelrede.

Whither tends th' expiring fate of England:
what destiny menaces the Britans;
Th' insulting enemy violating
Their league overruns all; and maks ye earth
weepe great flouds of blood, drunk with ye current
w.ch flowes from wounded, slaughterd carcasses:
Rivers are purpled, and roughly glide along
Their ready banks hasting to the Ocean
As witnesses of misery. alas!
wee have bin Britans; but that name must be
eraz'd,

[Dedicatory Letter to *Alfrede or Right Reinthron'd*:]

To [fol. 1]

The most deseruing Lady.

y^{e} Lady Blounte.

Madam

'Twas with no small difficulty that I obtained this vacancy of my thoughts wch with reluctancy admit y^{e} entervalls of ex=[/]terne cogitations, holding it schismaticall to communicate with any other obiect then what they are wedded to; y^{e} Arguments I vsed of passing away the time, and diverting Malencholy had bin of no validity had they not been seconded with an engagement that what'ere I applyed my ffancy to should bee intended as an Offering consecrated to you their sole employment: But this devotion brings not y^{e} obligation of throwing away so much time as to reade it, I rather beg the contrary, though I confesse y^{r} ingenu=[/]ity hath this satisfactory advantage, that it can represent to your intellect not what is, but what should haue bin written: vpon this presumption I am encouraged [fol. 1v] to[1] expose King Alfrede to y^{r} vew homely clad, and without the adventitious graces of pearles, diamonds, or any ornamentall jewells; in fine he is not accouter'd to receiue visits, his desire therefore is to live a Recluse immured perpetually within ye Cell of y^{r} Cabinet,[2] Or if y^{r} Curiosity prompt you to looke vpon him, and laugh at his ridiculous attire, shut y^{r} chamber dore least any stranger surprize him, and discouver his deficiency, and therein the weakenesse of

Madam

your most affectionate

Brother

R: K:

---

[1] Catchword for fols. 1–1v.

[2] "A small chamber or room; a private apartment, a boudoir"—*OED*, s.v. "cabinet."

Alfrede

or

Right Reinthron'd

Being

A

Tragi=comedie //

[fol.2]

The Names of y[e] Actors. [fol. 3][3]

S[t.] Cuthbert.—	-King Alfred's Patrone.
Alfrede.—	-King of england.
Edelvitha.—	-The queene.
Osberga.—	-The King's Mother.
Edward.—	-Eldest son to the King
Adelvold.—	-Youngest son to y[e] King.
Elfred[a].—	-Eldest daughter to y[e] King.
Elgine.—	-youngest daughter to y[e] King.
Humfrey.—	-Generall of the Horse.
Athelrede.—	-Generall of the ffoote.
Neothus.—	-A holy Ermite.
Denevulphe. Crabula.	-A Swin-heard. his wife.
Strumbo.—	-His Son.
Soldiers. Dancers.	
Gothurnus.—	-King of the Danes.
Osberne.—	-His Brother.
Gormo.—	-Kinsman to Gothurnus.
Rollo.	[-Officer to Gothurnus]
A Bragadocia.—	-Soldier to Gothurnus.
[Pimpo.—	-Servant to Bragadocia]
Pipero. Titmus. }—	-Pages to Gothurnus.
4 Messengers[.]	
Soldiers.	

[3] Fol. 2v is a blank page.

Alfrede. [fol. 3v]
or
Right reinthron'd.
a
Tragicomedie.

Prologue

S$^{t.}$ Cuthbert.

Who this deny's that Heau'n a pious care
Retains for humain things; that saints apeare
Cal'd to th' assistance of affaires below,
Must Cruelnesse ith' Deity allow,
That Mortall things without a Rule are hurl'd
And deeme those Spirits helplesse to y^{e} world:
Piety's no Captiue to the Orbs aboue
But oft vnto afflicted lands doth moue.
This makes me to forsake the glorious skyes
To visit my poore Cuntry wch exhausted lyes
A prey to Mars, where the inhuman Dane
with sacrilegîous Crueltys doth staine
Our holy Alters; but Im come to bring
Help to th' afflicted, mindfull of that King
Of my deare England, who zealously intent
so oft his prayres vnto my eares hath sent.
If ever you haue heard of Cuthberts Name
whom England nourished, now heav'n doth claime[.]
I the same now will true examples give [fol. 4]
How short, vnconstant, is ye life Men liue
which alwayes the divine P[r]otection wants
Obtained by the sacred prayres of Saints.
King Alfrede vanquished by adverse ffate
Now from the Danes seekes safety by retreate;

And he who yet nere knew but still t' or'ecome
Can from his foes scarce refuge find at home.
Thus heau'n to th' Britans punishment doth send,
Till thaught[4] by evells they their liues amend.
   Loe one oth Kings chiefe Captains doth apeare[;]
I goe; strait to return an Actor here.
   Beginnings clad in sorrows Livery
   will end in joy, content, alacrity.

Act: i

Scen: i.

Athelrede.

Whither tends th' expiring fate of England?
What destiny menaces the Britans?
Th' insulting enemy violating
Their league overruns all; and mak[e]s ye earth
weepe great flouds of blood, drunk with ye current
wch flowes from wonded,[5] slaughterd Carcases:
Rivers are purpl'ed, and roughly glide along
Their reedy banks hasting to the Ocêan
As witnesses of misery. Alas!
Wee haue bin Britans; but that name must be
eraz'd, and Cuntry too, by th' cruell Danes, [fol. 4v]
A Cuntry styl'd ye Nursery of Saints.
Why do I fly? Death's far more welcome
then to outliue the safety of my Cuntry.
Ile seeke the enimy, embrace a death
more glorîous from an adversaries hand.
O sad Relicks of my Cuntry! And you,
whose blacke embraces smoot[6] all things, dark night
I call to witnes; that no regard for life,
nor hopes of refuge from this dark vmbr[a]ge,

---

[4] That is, "thought."
[5] Variant of "wounded" used throughout MS.
[6] That is, "smote."

The Cowards shelter, hath excited me
to an ignoble flight; but that ye night
hath lost my enemys, tyr'd with Killing.
But who comes here?—

Scene. 2

Humfrey. Athelrede.

Where am I? How haue I thus lost ye King?
ATH: Tis Humfrey; I know his voice.
HUM: Shall I call out? The mercilesse Dane w^{ch}
ready arm'd surrounds ye whole wood will heare.
Shall I return? Night makes me ignorant
wch way to take. Shall I once more assault
the enemy? To dy alone brings noe
revenge; oh, cruell fates! O England!
Not to be found in thy selfe, whose sorrows
Are preludes of ioy to th' insulting foe.
ATH: Humfrey, make Athelrede y^{r} Associate [fol. 5]
in life or death. Lets hast in search oth' King.
Loe; here he comes, accompanied with
enter King.
the two Princes Edward and Adelvolde.

Scena. 3

Alfrede, Edward, Adelvolde,
Athelrede. Humfrey.

My knowledge of the Place tells me where
I am; this wood leades to the Isle Athelnea,
wither I direct my flight. Thou, deare Childe,
Make hast to Osberga, now glad to trust
Her safety to th' Assyle[7] of a deepe Pit,
And by thy Conduct let her follow me.
Run[;] it is requisite you make great hast.[8]
ADEL: My feete shall be swift, thô feare clogs my hart.

---

7 "The earlier form of ASYLUM"—*OED*, s.v. "Asyle."
8 Obsolete form of "haste" used throughout MS.

ALF: Edward, hast to thy mother[;] out run the winds[.]
Let the Castle be a Safegaurd to her
and thy Sisters; night will secure them thither.
Then cautiously returne alone to me.
ED: I'm all obediênce[;] y^r comãnds are don.
ATH: Alfrede permit y^r servants t'attend you.
HUM: Lets be associates in y^r flight, as well as griefe.
ALF: Who hopes for nothing needs not any friends.
ATH: A companion in misery is halfe a Cure.
ALF: He deales vnfriendly, that makes his friends partake
of's griefe: sorrows shall be my Companions.
Wherefore be gon[;] night will favour my designe
best alone: Humfrey if the safety of
y^r King hath any influênce vpon you [fol. 5v]
declare y^r fidelity by leauing
me alone. 'T will be the securest way[.]
To evade our enemies affaires here
will require y^r stay. From every part
o th' Kingdome levy forces. Embody[9]
Our dissipated troopes: then follow me
to Athelnea a place impregnable
to th' Enemy.
HUM: I hast to your Comãnds.
exit
ALF: Nor shall a test of thy fidelity
Athelrede, be wanting, if my Commands
you'l follow.
ATH: Tis done what ere you bid.
ALF: Here take this Crowne, a burthen too heavy,
A glory fatall sometimes to the owner:
I deliver it to thy custody[;]
Let some safere place secure it till heau'n
disrobe Alfrede of his dire Miseries;
then accompa[ny]ing[10] Humfrey come to me.
ATH: A faithfull hand shall execute y^r commands.
exit
ALF: Now Alfrede, hauing lost thy Kingdome
put of[11] thy Kingly robes; and lay aside

---

[9] That is, to bring into one body.

[10] Employed as an adjective meaning, "The action of being a companion. . . . Acting as a companion, going along with"—*OED*, s.v. "accompanying."

[11] Variant of "off" used throughout MS.

that hatefull Purple whose too much splendor
will serve but to betray thee to thy ffoes.
Thus Metamorphis'd by this habit
Puts on ye habit of a common soldiers
into a common soldier, I haue lost
all envy: Ambition dyes when not fed
with this Regall burthen. Poverty is [fol. 6]
lay's his robes in a pit
in no place regarded. In this recesse
lyes hid the King. Thus gold most fit's inhum'd;[12]
and the bright luster of Purple cover'd[,]
with whose poysenous glory sweld Kings oft
breake forth into the byles[13] of tyranny.
But my designe forbids delays, Complaints
Must not vsurpe that time wch safety wants:
exit

Sce: 4.

Gothurnus, Osbernus. Gormo.
Bragadocia, Pimpo. soldiers.
Pipero. Titmus.

O sluggards in y^{r} iust Rage! Vnmindfull
Of revenge! Hath feare of Killing ceas'd[14] y^{r}
victorious hands? Why drown yee not this
hostile Cuntry in its owne bloud? Ere this
A sanguine deluge flowing from the dead,
should haue baptis'd this land, A purple Sea.
O sloathfull Soldiers! Fearefull! Even then
when Mars invites you to a rich Booty.
The groanes of gasping bodyes, are musicke
to my eares. Tis my delight to behold
expiring Countenances. Tis no mercy
to spare an enimy. Do yee demur?
Hast, hast, take ye to y^{r} Armes. Throw firebrands
On all the land. And let a vaporous smoke

---

[12] Interred, buried in the earth.

[13] Figuratively, "Anger, ill-temper, peevishness"—*OED*, s.v. "bile."

[14] Transitively, "To put a stop to the action of others, a state or condition of things, to stop"—*OED*, s.v. "cease."

vmbrage[15] its Cities. The hand that giues death
To Alfrede shall be rewarded with [fol. 6v]
A thousand pounds. Brother Osberne, and you
Gormo my deare Kinsman, pursue the flying
Enemy. Let ev'ry hand be animated
vnto slaughter: human bloud, a witnesse
of my rage, shall pay a dreadfull tribute
to the Ocean.

OSB: Let it: and by this hand shall fall, what'ere
hath hitherto bin fear'd by Danish Kings.

exit

GOR: Lets March: Ile heape destruction vpon houses,
and ruinate Cities. The palenesse of
the rising day prophesies desolation
but setting shall depart with sanguine markes.

BRA: Squire advance: let me blow downe Kingdoms
with my breath, and blow vp townes. To day
Not one lesse then thirty-thousand, shall be
sacrifis'd to my indignation.
Every blow shall send a Heccatombe
for a present to Pluto.

PIM: That is, with one blow hee'l slay a hundred
men, altho with a hundred blows he shall
ne're kill one.

exit Bra: Pim:

GOTH: Goe, goe, be gon: let our Dominions spring
from English bloud; England I rise from thy ashes
As a Phœnix from his reviving fflame;
Thy bloud shall Kingdoms hatch t'encrease my fame

exit

Sce: 5.ª # [fol. 7]

Osberga. Adelvolde.

O wretched state of life! Why fly'st thou death
Osberga? A queene, a mother of Kings?
Now a vagabond, to be pitied
even by thy enimies. Why doe I
Protract that life, whose end will also be

---

[15] In the literal Latin sense of "cast a shadow over."

A period to so many Miseries?
Alas! Death would be lesse painfull to me
then a life, wch hath seene my Son disthron'd,
and fertile Britain groaning vnder
th' oppression of a cruel tyrant.
What other misery can befall me?
ADEL: Why loose you time with sighing griefe?
Lets rather fly. The enemy aproaches,
sweld with fury, and thirsting after bloud:
this, this way, will bring vs to my ffather[.]
These woods will afford a sanctuary.
OSBE: Think'st thou by death, death can be avoyded?
Cal'st thou that life which breath[e]s nothing but woe?
Goe, follow thy father; I haue resolv'd
to end a life grown old with afflictions.
Death from th' enimy will prevent a more
cruell one, springing from those pensiue yeares
my griefe presages. Liue thou; to revenge
thy father[,] whose Kingdome from thy brother
may once descend to thee. I'm already
Inanimate; griefe hath stupifyed [fol. 7v]
my ioynts. Goe; 'tis rest not death that I seeke.
ADEL: O forget not my ffather, me, y^{r} selfe!
You were wont by y^{r} advice to comfort
my ffather, when oprest with care; who now
shall doe you that office? you vs'd to say
it is impious to accelerate death.
Why seeke you to be y^{r} owne Murtherer?
Lets fly: life onely thus can be preserv'd.
But if you haue determin'd to embrace
death: let Adelvold associate[16] you:
if you choose life, Ile be y^{r} leader;
if death y^{r} companion. Rather elevate
y^{r} Spirits oprest with evells in which
to be orecome is the greatest evell.
OSBE: Pardon me, deare Childe, that am halfe senseles;
Raging griefe had almost got th' vpper hand,
and made me not myselfe. But now sorrow
is banish't from my brea[s]t: and I'm restor'd
vnto my selfe; I search not after death,
Nor now do I feare to prolong my life.

---

[16] In modern English, "accompany."

Goe, ile follow; fly, Ile persue; wherere
you moue to seeke y^{r} father, Ile search there.

Sce: 6.

Humfrey.

Tis strange! No place is exemp't from the noyse
of enimies; nor doth th' obscurity
of the night retard their persute.
Wherere I goe I'm sure to meete with foes.
Tis more then once that troopes haue lodg'd me round, [fol. 8]
yet by th assistance of the night I've 'scap'd.
Goe, or stay; tis equally perilous.
If I goe, their torches will discover me,
for all the fyld's one flame, wch vsurping
Element makes a bright day in spight of night;
if I stay, or hide myselfe, no place ith' wood
is left vnsearch't. Their lights will soone betray
the most obscure recesse. Another way
Must be invented; This garment wch I Know
to be some Dane's came most fortunately
into my hands; I lately tooke it from
a dying soldier. Ile put it on,
then passing for a dane, I shall more facilly
encounter some surer meanes to escape.
But I'm betraid, sombody comes hither[;]
my sword shall end his iourney. Hold. It may be
some friend, and not an enemy, I feare.

Sce: 7.

Athelrede, Humfrey.

Alas! How I am tost, 'twixt feare and Cares.
I am pursued by my enemies
not much vnlike the hunted lieveret[17]
wch to secure her flight meander-like
runs into doubles to delude the dogs[,]

[17] A young hare, especially one in its first year—*OED.*, s.v. "leveret."

yet by her feet's known s[c]ent betray's herselfe:
Is't life I care for? No, tis dearer far
then life; the Kingdoms glory; Alfrede's Crowne.
Death's sooner to be embrac't then this should [fol. 8v]
fall into the enimies hand. I heare
th aproach of souldiers; their Armour makes
A noyse. My anxious mind's vncertaine
How, or where to dispose of Englands Pledge.[18]
A doubtfull feare possesses me, whither
losse of Crowne, or life is to be chosen;
Let life be lost; so't purchase This security.
HUM: O trusty ffaithfulnesse! Humfrey why dos't
thou thus deliberate? Cans't suffer one
so generous, and a ffriend, to perish[,]
whom with these cloaths thou may'st saue; and a Crown too[?]
What can acrew[19] from thy private safety
equallising the losse thy Cuntry,[20] and
thyselfe will sustaine,[21] if destitute
of helpe thou lets't so stout a Captaine dy:
My soule thou hast breath'd enough, tis time to dye,
not ingloriously if by an enemy.
Thy Cuntry's ruine, and thy King exil'd,
the earth bedew'd with english bloud, thy flight
desperate, thy life a theater of griefs;
these and a thousand vnborn miseries
will be the obiects of a sadder life;
Hope can suggest no reliefe—Tis resolv'd.
These cloaths shall be for him—what, yet in doubt?
Deliberation now's degenerous.[22]
Dost feele reluctancy to saue a friend?
'Twill be a glory, cheape if at th' expence
of thy owne life. Here, ffaithfull Athelrede
Receiue a safety iust now despear'd of; [fol. 9]
Put on these danish cloath's: let this disguise
gives Ath: ye danes cloaths
taken from an enemy protect both
y^{r} life and Crowne. More time I dare not spend.

---

[18] Alluding to Alfred's crown.

[19] That is, "accrue."

[20] That is, "the loss *of* thy country."

[21] Object implicit: "thyself will sustain the loss of thy country."

[22] Used throughout MS to mean, "Fallen from ancestral virtue or excellence, unworthy of one's ancestry or kindred, degenerate"—*OED*, s.v. "degenerous."

Farewell. Be mindfull of y^{r} dying friend.

exit

Sce: 8.

Athelrede.

Oh: stay: depart not yet. Returne. Hee's fled,
most inocent, to death; and tis for me;
Prodigall of his owne life to bestow't
on me; he bids me live that he may dye.
Is life so sweet? Is death so full of gall?
No, no, Ile rush on death, and call him backe:
but where shall I search? Whither follow him?
Hee's far from hence, but too neare his owne death.
He robs himselfe to furnish mee with life.
Oh cruell piety! I'me left to wade
through miseries, wch death will free him from.
But must he dye? Ile rather shew the way.—
What shall I at last resolve? Life or death.
If death; I loose my trust the crown. If life
A friend. My Cuntry bids me liue, piety
Commands me dye. Let life then be my choise,
the Kingdom's good, and Alfrede exact it.
Wherefore this disguise shall make me a stranger
to my selfe. Fortune I hope may Humfrey
safely give, and me my friend: tis fit
sometimes by such deceits to temporize[.]
Ile yet retaine the shelter of ye wood, [fol. 9v]
till metamorphis'd by these cloaths, I march
amid'st the Enimy, with hopes to finde
occasions to declare my gratefull minde.

exit

Sce: 9.

Osberne. Souldiers.

Souldiers bring y^{r} lighted torches hither.
Let not a corner be vnsearch'd. Who'ere

snatches a torch from one of ye sol.

it was that ye darke night protected from

my hands, shall not long escape my persute:
He cant be far. Search ev'ry hole, descend
into the caues oth' wood: beset it round,
he hath provok'd vs, and must be punisht
or vaine were Osbern's Rage. What dark refuge
is he got into? Or hangs he in the clouds,
suspended by the eares? Why trifle ye?
Let y^r lights make day ev'ry where apeare[;]
hee'l scarce make a second escape. Should Joue
protect him, i'de fetch him thence. Ile ruine
and consume to ashes all round about
ffire or sword shall find this villain out.

exit

Sce: 10.

Gormo. Humfrey. Souldiers.

Hum-bound

Bring the Captiue hither: death shall teach him
the weight of my hand. but one life's too poore
a victime for my fury. This sword, could it
meete with as many opposers should send
Thousands to Pluto. Tis a happinesse [fol. 10]
My adversaries are wont to striue for;
tis a glory thou dy'st by Gormo's hand.
If britan's harts can yet afford any blood,
Now prepare thy breast.—
HUM: Behold it naked; strike.
GOR: FFirst Ile know thy Name, and extraction.
HUM: My Name is Humfrey: my birth not ignoble
descended from illustrious Ancestors,
and now Generall of Alfred's fforces.
GOR: Tis well. Ile preserve him for a Ransome:
However Ile first try his Courage. *aside*

runs at him with his naked sword

GOR: Art thou not afraid? HUM: Of what?
GOR: Of death. HUMF: Twill be an end of misery.
GOR: Thou shalt dye. HUM: Tis most certain.
GOR: And by my hand. HUM: I desire it.
GOR: What to dye? HUM: For my King.
GOR: He's nowhere. HUM: Hee's in his Kingdome.
GOR: But exil'd. HUM: FFor his ffaith.

GOR: What faith: HUM: The Christian.
GOR: What does that benefit you with? HUM: Salvation.
GOR: In death? HUM: In the death of Christ.
GOR: To wit, A Man. HUM: And God.
GOR: What did he make? HUM: The world.
GOR: Of what? HUM: Of nothing.
GOR: For whom did he make it? HUM: For man.[23]
GOR: And Man, for whom? HUM: FFor himselfe.
GOR: What did he doe? HUM: Dye.
GOR: And yet a god? HUM: The worlds redem[p]tion.
GOR: By dying? HUM: By louing.
GOR: Whom? HUM: His enemies. [fol. 10v]
GOR: Where? HUM: vpon the Crosse.
GOR: What was his offence? HUM: His inocence.
GOR: What compeld him? HUM: Iniquity.
GOR: Whose? HUM: Mans.
GOR: Thou telst vs strange things were they not fables.
But I wonder [a] lyar should be so
pious. Behold now thy fate aproaches.
HUM: I'le not decline it.
GOR: Liue then but Know tis my gift.

Sce: 11.

Osberne. Gormo. Humfrey.
souldiers.

Gormo that Captiue you haue manicle'd
By my industry alone became a Prey.
GOR: But by my Art became a Prisoner.
OSB: A Beast once found is easily taken.
GOR: This was easy to be found.
OSB: The night shelter'd him.
GOR: I tooke him in the night.
OSB: Scarse daring so much ith day.
GOR: I dare doe anything ith day that Osberne dares.
OSB: Resigne the Prisoner.
Or learne by fighting the vigour of my Arme:

---

[23] Reminiscent of Dr. Faustus's catechismic response to Mephistophilis's contention that man is more glorious than heaven: "If heaven was made for man, 'twas made for me!" (*Dr. Faustus*, II.ii.10) [*The Complete Plays of Christopher Marlowe*, ed. Irving Ribner (New York: Odyssey Press, 1963).]

GOR: If thou could'st thunder out Joues light'ning
And throw it at me, I'd countermeete[24] it.
they prepare to fight

Sce: 12. # [fol. 11]

Gothurnus. Osberne. Gormo.
Humfrey. Attendants.

Whats this I see? My Captaines duelling?
Here Gormo, there Osberne, hasting vnto
their owne destruction? What ist that breeds
Such rage, exasperated by some mistake.
OSB: This Prisoner pursu'd by me ith' Night
Gormo most iniuriously detaines.
GOR: I ignorant of what had past ith Night
by accident discover'd him after
his escape from Osberne.
OSB: This hand forc't him to a flight[.]
GOR: This compel'd him to a rendition.
OSB: My labour discoured[25] him.
GOR: Mine tooke him.
GOTH: Is this th incentiue of so great a Crime?
provoking Kinsmen to their bloudy swords.
Is the regard of blood of Amity so vile
not to impede your rash hands from
throwing to the ground yr) new built trophies?
O vnparalel'd! Vnheard of Madnesse.
How neere we are loosing quite that Kingdome,
where till now we had fixt so sure a footing.
What inconsulted[26] rashnesse hath made you
forget me, yr selves, yr cuntry, all things?
If yr Courage prompted you to slaughter[,] [fol. 11v]
yr enemies might haue bine[27] its obiect.
If you covet Kingdoms, ye vanquish't Britans
make you a Resignement:[28] ist honours you

---

[24] "To match (in opposition); to checkmate"—*OED*, s.v. "countermate."

[25] That is, "discovered."

[26] "Unconsulted, not asked"; also, "inconsult," meaning "inconsiderate, unadvised, unreflecting"—*OED*, s.v. "inconsulted."

[27] That is, "been."

[28] Meaning, "the act of resigning."

Aspire to? Y^{e} glory of y^{r} conquest
affords it. Ist riches you desire?
All England yealds a spoile to y^{r} triumphs.
What seeke you more? Are you yet thirsty of
mutuall blood? O wickednesse, abhor'd
Even by Infernalls. What greater Plague
Could Alfrede wish the Danes then what y^{r} selves
are authors of. Recall. O readmit
y^{r} pristine amity, and turn y^{r} rage
vpon y^{r} enimies. Sheath vp y^{r} swords
and Anger too. Let friendships firmest leagues
vnite y^{r} harts. Shake hands, embrace, tis well.
they embrace
Slight mistakes obtaine an easy pardon.
Conquerors should allwayes hold togeather.
GOR: Osberne; in signe of friendship this Captiue
I resigne to y^{r} dispose.
OSB: Y^{r} gift shall be to th' King
least I seeme partiall in my owne cause[.]
Nobody is a iust Judge to himselfe.
GOTH: I accept the gift and shall reward
y^{r} merits. Now, to th' worke in hand.
FFollow y^{r} victory, leaue no time for flight
A Captaine ought to Know how to pursue[,]
as well as overcome. Goe you before[.] [fol. 12]
exeunt osb: Gor:
Ile follow with the body oth' Army.

Sce: 13.

Gothurnus. Humfrey. Athelrede
disguis'd. Rollo.

Now, bring hither the Plotter of all this
Mischiefe, that he may feele my vigorous hand.
By his sad example others shall know
what tis t' incensse the fury of a King.
Was thou the Cause then of my Captains quarrel[,]
so neere spilling each others blood[?]
And art thou yet vnpunisht by Gothurnus?
Now call vpon thy God to thy reliefe[.]
He shall scarce deliver thee from my Hands.
HUM: Cease thus blasphemously to excite him

to thy owne punishment whose thunder shakes
the trembling world, whose Awfull Nod
Moues the Celestiall Orbes, and guides the whole
ffabrick of the Vniverse. Tis he that
enthrones Kings, and precipitates Tyrants
from their vsurped glory. You are ignorant
how great a Deity you haue provok'd.
GOTH: Let thy God thunder, and throw light'ning too[.]
My iust rages sayes thou shalt dye.
ATH: O stay the fatall blow Most gracious Prince,
till I shall relate ye story of my Misfortune
occasion'd by his most barbarous hand
that now stands here guilty of punishment[.]
If you shall perceive my request is iust
grant an easy condescention to it.
GOTH: Speake quickly then. Rage brookes not long delays[.] [fol. 12v]
ATH: Wee were three brothers owning the same father
all fighting vnder y^r glorious ensignes.
This bloody villaine depriv'd me of my
ffather and both my brothers[,] invoking[29]
with their dying words the iust gods, to be
Revengers of that Crime and periury.
Hauing orecome my ffather by deceit,
he promis'd him his freedome, if bought
with the Captivity of two of his sons:
they, most ready to preserve their ffather,
with an vnanimous resolution
Commit themselves to fortune; These two became
Death's prey. I'm onely vnfortunately left
to vndergoe the worst of miseries;
He, as soone as he had got these Pledges
for my deare ffather perfidiously
laughing, here said he, take y^r father w^{ch}
you haue redeem'd. Withall taking his sword
into his hand, (vnhear'd of Cruelty!)
strikes of my ffathers head in ye presence
of his two sons: The head besmear'd wth blood
tumbles vpon the ground. These spectators
were struck with amazement: their blood somtimes
retiring into hidden Arteries
Caus'd Palenesse like a waue by reciprocall

[29] That is, "my brothers, who invoked."

turns, to overspread their Countenances.
Nor is [t]here an end of his Cruelty;
ffor this salvage[30] Tygre not contented
to period his rage with my ffathers death,
Most inhumanly with his sword cuts of[f] [fol. 13]
both the heads of his dutifull Ofspring.
Alas! What griefe possest my breast at this
sad obiect? What sighs did I then send forth?
Now, my Liege, let me beg this one request
vpon my Knees; that he who murthered[.]

Kneels

My father, and my Brothers, may receive
a death from my hand, correspondent to
so immense a wickednesse[,] least a death
from y^{r} victorious arme should make him
desirous of so glorious an end.
GOTH: Tis granted. Prepare some new invented
torment that Plalaris[31] may glory to
call it his; excogitate[32] something more
Horrid then the Roare of a brazen Bull.
Let ev'ry groane be a Memorandum
of thy ffathers, and brothers Cruell death.
Rollo, be thou spectator of his death,
garded by a band of souldiers, and bring
his head fastned vpon a speare to me.
This my Command vnlesse fullfild I see
My pleasure is you all shall hanged bee.

exit

Sce: 14.

Rollo. Souldiers. Athelrede
Humfrey.

Come Souldiers. Lets faithfully execute
Our Charge; thô me-thinkes tis somthing severe.

---

[30] Obsolete form of "savage" used throughout MS.

[31] Phalaris. Cruel autocrat of Acragas, legendary for roasting his victims alive in a brazen bull—*OCD*, s.v. "Phalaris." Machiavel in Marlowe's *The Jew of Malta* invokes Phalaris and his brazen bull (Prologue, 23–24).

[32] "To think out; to construct, frame, or develop in thought; to contrive, devise"—*OED*, s.v. "excogitate."

Let thousands of our enemys confront vs
and with a hundred Troopes surround vs,
The vncontroled vallour of the Danes [fol. 13v]
Knows how to resist oposing ffortune.
Vertue shines most in a doubtfull Attempt;
and Courage most generous, when shunning
the base delays of feare, a desperate
designe difficultly crownes the victor.
Goe on then securely with y^r revenge;
determine whether a suddain or a
lingring death shall dispatch him: whether
y^r hand, or some ones else shall give the blow:
tis no matter how, so his death be sure.

ATH: I haue resolv'd the manner. My revenge
shall correspond with his dire wickednesse.
The same way my ffather, and my brothers
lost their liues, shall also his destroy.
A sword shall doe't. If thou desirest to
speake, or with thy vltimate breath invoke
Any deity; dispatch it quickly.

HUM: Dos't thou preach Piety? And exhort
Religion which thou never knew thyselfe?
Thus guilty of the greatest wickednesse:
dost thou then belieue that there is a God,
and dos't not Know he is thy Enimy?
Who hast been the author of all this deceit,
whereby my life and fame are like to perish
without pleading for my owne inocence[?]
I a periur'd Person? Pray in what place
did I commit this bloody Cruelty?
Why turn'st thou aside? Shew here thy guilty
Countenance. But to what end do I speake?
Is't not to insensible Brutes I send [fol. 14]
my Complaints? Goe happyly on My Soule,
despising death; receive a double triumph
flowing from Martyrdome and inocence.
O Christ the Author of all Piety;
thou eternall Happinesse to the iust,
bestow that reward which thou hast promis'd
to Champions of the Christian ffaith.

ATH: Tis enough. Before thou go'st a Victime
to my ffathers Manes,[33] take this Massage,[34]

---

[33] In one of its meanings, "the 'shade' of a departed person, considered as an

whispers to Hum: and gives him a sword and vnbinds him
which thou from me shall tell him secretly
Humfrey takes this sword. Tis Athelrede bids
ioyne y^{r} force to his. If fate deny vs
life, at least wee'l dy togeather.
HUM: I follow y^{r} Advice and you.
ROL: Treason. Wee are betray'd—
they fly vpon Rol: who falls
ye rest run away.
HUM: Their Captaine being slain[,] ye rest are fledd[.]
Now let me embrace the deare Preserver
of my life.
ATH: Humfrey (a Name more capacious then friend)
to thee I returne that life thou wast
A doner[35] of to me. I should haue been
vngratefull not to haue restor'd it.
Pardon my loue if I haue iniured
y^{r} Name, by a fraudulent but pious
Calumniation.
HUM: Such an offence brings its pardon with it.
Tis now vnsecure to stay here longer.
ATH: Lets therefore hast away.—
.exeunt

Sce: 15. # [fol. 14v]

Rollo. ~

Rollo rises

A thousand Divels goe along with you!
Are we then betray'd by this dissembling
villaine? How nere was I the stygian lake!
How little did I want, quite voyde of sense,
from Knocking at grim Pluto's gate! I haue
No wound that's mortall; yet I was something
stupify'd with the blow. Now what's to
be don? If I goe to th' King I'm sure
to dye. My head will pay for the offence;

---

object of homage or reverence, or as demanding to be propitiated by vengeance"—*OED*, s.v. "manes."

[34] That is, "message."

[35] Meaning "donor."

and for a Britain I shall be sacrific'd
to Gothurnus his ffury. But the Gods
And our owne Nature teacheth vs not to
Cast away our liues. And wee haue so much
Reason, not to fling ourselves into
the hands of a powerfull Enemy.
He armes his enemy, that forewarn's him;
so Gothurnus threat'ning the penalty
I must vndergoe[,] if I fulfil'd not
his Commãnds, hath preserved me from it.
I know his disposition's rigid,
And his Anger mercilesse, when incens't.
Wherefore if I returne I runne my necke
into the halter. If fly; I throw myselfe
vpon the enemy. Ther's yet a meane
to be experienced.— It shall be soe.
I'le to those souldiers which feare hath dispers't
And the same Cause and Offence hath made my [fol. 15]
ffellow-Criminalls. Ile recall them to
their Armes. And vpon yonder hill ith' midst
o th' wood, wee'l get our liuing by robery;
vntill made rich with booties we apease
our offended King with presents; these will
reingratiate vs; where supplications
find a repulse: these force an easy way.
The Temple of Reliefe Gold opens strait[;]
Let nere so strict a Porter Keepe the gate.

exit

Act: 2.

Sce: i.

Edelvitha. Elfrede.
Elgine.

What a Band of feares allarums my breast
In ev'ry part? As a Tree summon'd
By the musicke of a whisp'ring Zephyr,

while its leauy[36] Haires periwigs[37] the ground,
seemes to dance; and throw itselfe into y^{e}
sporting armes of the soft embracing winds:
and vnconstant now receives the Kisses
of the south; now those of the Northern wind:
Or else is batred[38] with a shower of Haile
And then grow's big into its owne ruine[,] [fol. 15v]
so my anxious mind with the least rumour
is tost with griefe; as the sea is impulst
by diversity of tempestuous waues.
I am a wretched obiect fortune sports
withall[,] fearing the Danes least my husband
by some stratagem fall into their hands:
and he become a Captiue to his foes,
Or I left a disconsolate widdow
to the cruelty of Barbarians;
what stormes of miserie will then menace
you my chiefest Care! Our onely hope whilst
prosperous; and Kingdoms beauty in spight
of all adversity. How rigidly
the mercilesse Enimy will then treat you!
Nor will his hatred be appeasd vntill
he hath prey'd vpon y^{r} virgine Purity.
ELF: Heav'n protect vs from so great a Mischiefe.
And yet I tremble with an inward feare
proceeding from a Dreame I had last night.
Sleepe had scarse stole away the day, and vaild
my eyes with night when pensively me thought
I wander'd in the vmbrage of a wood:
A horrour lodg'd ith' trees excited feare
wch mou'ed by the wind made a dolefull noise,
whilst the courting winds play'd with ye green leaues[,]
when on a suddain from the one side rushes
Out a Leopard[,] from the other a Beare[,] [fol. 16]
both with horrible roares making towards me:
but seeing their Prey stand dubious to which
it should be due; like light'ning they return
their Rage to on[e] another, and with a stout
Combat they dispute the victory:

---

[36] Adjectival plural for "leaves"; cf. modern "leafy."
[37] Used poetically as a verb.
[38] That is, "battered."

I like a Statue, made immovable
by excesse of feare stood still, to be
The Conquerors Prize[,] when my first enimy
the Beare, roaring with a wound received
from his adversary falls to the ground.
The victor presently lays claime to me,
to be dismember'd by his ravenous teeth:
But behold[,] vnexpectedly a young
Lion comes forth of the adiacent wood
and demanding me renews the Combat,
and soone becomes the Leopards Conqueror.
Here sleepe tooke flight, and left my anxious mind
oprest with feare of some portended ill.
ELG: This night also represented to me
A most dreadfull imagination;
ffancy gaue me the prospect of a high rock
Neare which a river did gently glide along=
the murmuring pibles:[39] a verdent plaine
beautify'd the vally[,] sylver'd ore with
the thin streames of meandricall[40] waters.
By chance a young Lambe following its dame
for sucke, did here commence its wanton plays. [fol. 16v]
The aire was cleare, the day without a Cloude,
Made pleasant by a gentle breath of wind;
The dewy grasse affording fresher bits
might cause their straying, or[e] the shady trees,
where couch't they found a shelter from ye heate.
The Sun had travail'd iust halfe his iourny,
And droue his Chariot to the highest pitch,
vewing the Center of ye world with a
perpendicular eye. The winds were still,
Nor did the Nightingall, that Syren
of the wood[,] chant forth its sweet Melodies,
Nor any bird broke silence with a Note;
when a suddain horror invests the place;
A dreadfull tempest from the clouded North
benights the day: light'ning broke thorow[41]
the condensed clouds; thunder (mixt wth raine)
Not much vnlike a Cannon furrowed

[39] Variant form of "pebbles."
[40] Meaning "meandering."
[41] In modern English, "through."

the ground, and shoke the Center of ye earth.
Immediately from an open vallie,
hedg'd on each side with the imbracing wood,
A Heard of wolves most dreadfully howling
rush forth, and opening their ravenous iawes,
make at both ye Dame and young one too.
Behold, this hungry troope had now impal'd
ye inocent Couple, trembling at their
approaching slaughter. In the interim
Two dogs breake from the oposite vally, [fol. 17]
and swiftly run vpon the salvage wolues[,]
Leauing the Prey to perfect liberty.
My sleepe then vanisht from me, and with it
my hopes of seeing what th' event would be.
EDEL: Dreames, the interpreters of afflicted Minds,
ffeede the senses with new shapes of evells;
And ffancy often represents what most
wee feare. But My Son comes in hast towards vs.

Sce: 2.

Edelvitha, Elfrede, Elgine
Edward.

What Newes brings he? His Countenance forespeakes
some ill: griefe sits characterd vpon
his cloudy forhead. Speake, what ist? What silent?
Tis enough. Thou hast learnt to speake too well
even by saying Nothing; now if thou
never speakest I know thy language.
Alfred's dead—

she faints

ELF: O brother, Sister, lend y^r helpe, she falls.
EDW: Resume y^r strength, deare Mother, I bring not
as you suppose, newes of my ffathers death.
Nor is he vanqusht yet, he liues not lesse
in Courage then th' insolent Gothurnus.
Hauing lost the victory, he is gone
ffor Refuge to the Isle Athelnea:[42]
wherefore provide for safety by y^r flight:

---

[42] Athelney, the marshy island on which Alfred made his stronghold in 878.

Night will further y^{r} escape, an'd I'le beare
you Company and be your Giude.[43] [fol. 17v]
EDEL: Alas! What Refuge can we hope, that may
promise a defence from the Enimy?
EDW: There stands a Castle plac't vpon a hill
which Nature hath surrounded with a Rocke:
nor is it far from hence, lets fly to that.
EDEL: Thou bidst vs seeke new miseries. I see
the Name of Great's but an empty sound.
I once was happy, now with woe oprest
And strait shall in my former nothing rest.

exeunt

Sce: 3.

Alfrede,
in the habit of a Comõn soldier.

Who makes a Crowne, beset with thornes of Cares,
His Idoll and fancies the splendor of his scepter
the lookinglasse of all glory; nor feares
the proteous vicissitude[44] of ffortune:
Let Alfrede, once King of England, be his
Obiect; now alone, without wife, Children,
Or his Army; wanting both his Kingdome,
and a place of Residence. Alas! From
what degree of happinesse am I fallen?
I haue had the triall of all fortunes,
that wch seats vs in a Throne, is as much
to be despis'd, as that wch pulls vs downe
to be lamented. The victorious Dane
like an encreasing Hydra[45] grows great
with my Ruine; A faithlesse Nation,
vnmindfull of their League,[46] A worshiper [fol. 18]
of false Gods, inhuman, delighting in
destruction, and a enimy to Peace:
One that hath bin so oft a Supplicant,

---

[43] That is, "guide."
[44] Knightley's not Drury's Latinizing pedantry here.
[45] Fabled hundred-headed monster.
[46] One of several allusions to material recorded by the Anglo-Saxon chroniclers on the Danes' breaking their treaty with Alfred.

and treated as a guest, is now become
an Insulter in our Teritories.
O Thou whose potent hand disposeth Crownes,
whose awfull Rod giues destiny to Kings,
put some end to thy Chastisements, nor let
perpetuall punishments attend our ffaults.
Be mercifull to thy belieuing fflocke,
disquieted on ev'ry side with an
Enimy defil'd with prophane worship.
Let the Criminall expiate his Crime,
and ffidelity at length triumph ore
the fraudulent Perfidy of the Danes.
Sombody is Coming hither—

Sce: 4.

Strumbo with a wallet.
Alfrede.

My breast trembles for feare like a quagmyre, my hart goes pit=a-pat, my belly rumbles, and lets of[f] horrible Reports, my stomach croakes, my head whisses,[47] my legs shake as if they were allready preparing to runne away. As Argus was all eyes so I am all eares, so that the least noise almost strikes me into a dead sownd.[48] Thus whilst I feare the Name of war abroad, I find it round about me, nor do the Danes[49] that are absent terrify me so much as I that am [fol. 18v] present who am my own executioner.

ALF: This fellow is the true interpreter of his degenerous Minde.

STR: O that Men would follow my Counsell; first I would advise 'em to eat often, but to drinke oftner, verry seldome to chide, but never to fight: for I commend our word selling lawyers;[50] a sort of poeple that will vehemently wrangle, and fight desperately with words; but when it comes to blows, they are silent, nay patient=[/]ly endure it, and verry wisely too.

---

[47] Used intransitively to mean "to whistle, whizz, or wheeze"—*OED*, s.v. "whiss."

[48] Variant of "swound" equivalent of modern "swoon."

[49] Catchword for fols. 18–18v.

[50] Clearly an anachronistic satiric target.

ALF: Hold there. Nobody shews his wisdome in being beaten—

STR: Now if yee would Know why I came hither so late ith night; y^e^ must vnderstan[d] that tis my humour to imitate malencholy Cats that goe abroad very seldome, without it bee-[/]ith night to hunt for a Prey; and then with their Caterwalling they Meaw out very tragicall Notes. My chiefest designe is to passe away the night in eating and drinking, be=[/]cause the day is more dangerous; however mis=[/]take not, I am not altogeather exempted from feare and that in no low degree; for I still fancy the Danes to ly hid vnder those trees.

ALF: He that imagins trees to be warriers, what would he doe if he should see a band of Armed souldiers?

STR: Would y^e^ know who I am? My Name is Strumbo that Merry Blade, only son and heire of a fisherman,[51] or [fol. 19] swinheard, for my father is Jack of both trades. Our house stands hard by in the Moores, and is hid in the midst of a plat of Osyers:[52] but is verry convenient for fishing, ffor all this Island called A=[/]thelnea abounds with Rivers and Marishes.[53] But because I belieue yee dont Know what I haue in the wallet vpon my backe,[54] Ile tell ye but verry briefely[,] because like to fairyes and Hobgoblins I am afraid to heare the Cocks crow; and all's long of these hell-hounds the Danes, who make nothing to swallow downe whole Men as we do Pottage. Here I haue bread, boyl'd fishes, and a Cup of stingo,[55] I haue also flesh; butter and Cheese; if any of you are a hungry, or desire to sharpen his wit with good liquor, so that he be'nt a Dane, let him follow me to the taverne.[56]

ALF: Ile speake to him for I am both hungry and thirsty. Ho! You!—

STR: I'm vndon. Y^e^ Danes, ye Danes—

runs out. leaues his wallet

ALF: Hee's fled, but has left me ye spoyle.

---

[51] Catchword for fols. 18v–19.

[52] "A piece or area of ground (usually) of small extent, a patch;" like modern "plot"—*OED*, s.v. "plat." "Osyers" (or "osiers") are a species of willow.

[53] That is, "marshes."

[54] Cf. Shakespeare's "Time hath, my lord, a wallet at his back" (with reference to where the wallet was worn)—*Troilus and Cressida*, 3.3.145.

[55] "Strong ale or beer"—*OED*, s.v. "stingo."

[56] A merry anachronism.

Ile loose no time but fall to this homely banquet.
How vaine's the Name of King? What doth it now
opens ye wallet
Availe me t'haue held a scepter ponderous
with gold? Wher's now my Purple star'd wth gems?
Where is my Crowne that splendor of my head?
My golden throne wch darts rayes of luster
paralells to the other sunne, whither
Now is it vanished? Can a Regall
Dignity defend from hunger? Or the [fol. 19v]
Cold embraces of death? Can Maiesty
give remora's[57] to th' swift houres of time?
Or Command a Calme when the sea rages?
Why do we so temerariously,[58]
Ambition[59] Kingdoms, wch lost we deplore
with such resentment; seeming to lament
because depriv'd of this Lifes Misery.
As a ffly playing with the bright splendor
of a Candle, vncautiously Kisses
the flame wch at last is it's owne ruine
Soe Men with guilded Miseries delight;
And honours to destruction invite.

Sce: 5.

S$^{t.}$ Cuthbert in a beggers habit.
Alfrede.

The Gulfe of widemouth'd scilla[60] not halfe soe
greedily swallow's vp shipwract vessels;
Nor so many Græcians, when they floated
vpon the tempestuous Seas, were dash't
by the batteries of rough waues, against
the Ceraunean[61] Rockes: as this present life
is furnish't with dangers and Misfortunes.
FFortune as proudly insults over Kings

---

[57] "An obstacle, hindrance, impediment, obstruction"—*OED*, s.v. "remora."
[58] "With temerity, rashly"—*OED*, s.v. "temerariously."
[59] The word functions as a verb.
[60] Scylla, fabled six-headed, female sea-monster.
[61] From "ceraunite," a Greek derivative listed in *OED* meaning "thunderstone," sometimes employed to signify meteoric iron.

As Peasants; making sport with the world,
but oft proues to[o] vnkind a Playfellow:
Behold, King Alfred now wanders thorow
the desolate woods without Attendants;
Hauing onely star-light wch shews his way, [fol. 20]
Sit[s] on the earth dismantled of his glory,
and satisfyes his hunger with corse[62] Meates;
But heau'n takes care of humain things, and he
that trusts in it, needs not despeare of help:
It was by my aide, that Alfrede 'scap't his foes,
protected in the shelter of a wood;
'twas I Compeld this Rusticke 'gainst his will
to leaue him those prouisions which
he had design'd for some other place;
I haue now assum'd this beggars habit
to aske an Almes: I'le goe towards him.
ALF: Who art thou, cloath'd in tetter'd[63] Raggs?
CUTH: I am, as you see A Needy old Man,
and what's worse miserable, for I am
almost dead with the common dicease of
Hunger, whilst salvage beasts fill their panches[64]
with their accustomed nutriment.
ALF: Come neere, ffellows in Misery ought to be
Companions[;] Poverty makes thee
miserable, and riches[65] me. We call
as well those miserable that haue lost
their riches, as those that never had 'em.
Sit down by me; the grownd will afford vs
a tible,[66] and heau'n provide vs meat.

---

[62] Variant of "coarse."

[63] A "tetter" or "tetters" is "A general term for any pustular herpetiform eruption of the skin, as eczema, herpes, impetigo, ringworm, etc."—*OED*, s.v. "tetter." Hence, "tetter'd Raggs" suggests clothing that bespeaks this condition.

[64] Variant of "paunch," meaning in this context, "The belly, abdomen; the stomach, as the receptacle of food"—*OED*, s.v. "paunch."

[65] That is, "enriches."

[66] That is, "table."

Sce: 6.

Strumb: S$^{t.}$ Cuthbert. Alfrede.

Stru: peepes out.

Ah Strumbo, what a sad spectacle do'st thou behold? How miserably miserable[67] am I[,] who left but one, and [fol. 20v] now find two danish suckers of my english Aile[.] What shall I doe? If I trap[68] to get it from 'em I'm a lost Man. If I let 'em alone, 't will all be drunke of before I shall get a sup of it: I am resolv'd to perish, to prevent perishing. I had rather dy sweetly drinking then miserably without it. Wherefore I must venture vpon something.— Why doe I thus delay time, when thers so great need of hast: the Body of that tree wch stands behind them is hollow; Ile enter into it, if fortune do'nt crosse me. In this tower, if once I chance to get my aile, Ile set it to my Nose and leaue not one Sup[69] in the Bottle. Well, Ile do't.—

gets into the tree

Now I am in a Castle of defence.

CUTH: Let Heau'n speake my thankes.

ALF: And who must I give thanks to?

STR: To me.—

CUTH: Whats the greatest misery a pore man can endure?

STR: Tis thirst.

CUTH: By y^{r} meanes I haue overcome it.

STR: Let me do so too by yours.

CUTH: To wit, that mortall enimy Hunger.

STR: To wit, thirst that greater enimy.

CUTH: I am now satisfy'd with eating: I haue made a feast.

STR: And I a fast; for whose sake I dont Know. I am sure my mouth makes water being thus tantaliz'd.

CUTH: I must now returne from whence I came.

STR: I must stay yet to empty the Bottle.

CUTH: If you haue any Comãnd to impose vpon me, Ile [fol. 21] performe it.

ALF: All I request is that I haue y^{r} prayers.

CUTH: FFarewell, you shall haue them; The body of this

---

[67] Catchword for fols. 20–20v.

[68] That is, "lay a trap."

[69] Applied as a noun, meaning to ingest liquid, the root being related to modern "soup"—*OED*, s.v. "sup."

tree will instruct you farther.

exit

STR: I'm vndon. For this Man by his discovery hath already disembodied me, and the other will presently make me nobody; now what difference is there betwixt the body of this tree, and me who strait shall be nothing but a Body, I meane headlesse.

ALF: Why said he the Body of that tree will instruct you farther? Is there anybody peradventure hid there?

STR: A miserable wretch.

ALF: It may be ther's gold.

STR: It drops then from the Mine[70] of my britch.

ALF: Or ist some Monument set in this Place.

STR: The superscription will presently apeare,
Here lyes Strumbo etc.

ALF: Ile see what there is.

STR: O that I were a Hare! Now—now I perish oh!

ALF: Speake who art thou in the tree?

STR: I am an Oracle, but certainly foretelling my owne death.

ALF: FFeare Nothing, thou art safe, I am thy ffriend.

STR: My friend? You are a Dane.

ALF: I Know this voice, tis the ffellows that left me this provision. Come out[;] I am no Dane. Here take money for the meat I haue eaten.

STR: Whats this I heare? Are you not a Dane? And haue [fol. 21v]

peeps out of the tree.

you money for me too[?] In what region do I liue? Am I myselfe? Or haue I lost my senses?

gives str: some gold.

ALF: Recollect y^{r}selfe, tis Gold, tis y^{rs} and I am y^{rs}[.]

str:comes out of the tree

STR: O best of Men, let me embrace y^{r} ffeete. Here, here, bore it through, pull out this tongue[71] wch even now cald you a Dane. You are no Dane but 'twas I that wanted braine,[72] nor are you of spaine, Nor a Neopolitaine; what then are you? A Man of nobler straine.

ALF: Joy transports him beyound himselfe[.]

---

[70] Figuratively, "An abundant source of supply; a store from which (something specified) may be obtained"—*OED*, s.v. "mine."

[71] Boring a hold through the tongue was a feared punishment meted out to felons.

[72] That is, "lacked brains."

How he's delighted with gold and ravish't
at the sight of it? Poore ffellow, he
Considers not how miserable they are
who are in loue with Money.

STR: Here I stand, and there I am; plac't betwixt Thirst and Hunger, 'twixt Scylla and Charibdis,[73] that is my Gold and my Aile to divide me that I am dubious wch to prefer before the Other; whether this that is palpable, or that which is potable. Ile therefore vnite both into one; for you haue seene, how I haue got gold for my Aile[;] now I must get Aile for my Gold. And then this will become palpable, and this Potable.

Sce: 7.

Crabula. Strumbo. Alfrede.

CRA: Ho! Strumbo! Strumbo!

STR: What do I heare? Wo's me! Tis the voice of my old and toothlesse Mother.

CRA: Strumbo, Strumbo. Rogue, villain, where art?

STR: This is thunder and Light'ning. What shall I doe now? [fol. 22] I thought 'twas for something my buttocks itch't[;] I shall be flea'd[74] with rods in pisse. O that all this gold (as much as tis) could ransome me from her rage. I haue no way but to try once again the sanctuary of my old tree. Thou (my deare Bottle) shall goe along with me, to mitigate my sorrows. Now I coniure you to say nothing.

ALF: I will not—

STR: 'St, no more.

CRA: I am so weary I can scarce stand vpon my legs. I am so ou-out of breath, that I thinke I haue little left in my body. I haue a cough to so troublesome[75] that it almost shakes out all my teeth. I am as hoarse as an Asse in bawling after this bastardly villaine.

STR: To wit me, she recons[76] vp my titles. But what are you mother if I am a bastard?

---

[73] See note to 2.5.1. Charybdis was the treacherous whirlpool that stood opposite Scylla's cave.

[74] Dialectical form of "flayed"—*OED*, s.v. "flay."

[75] That is, "very troublesome."

[76] "To con again" or "recount"—*OED*, s.v. "recon."

CRA: If once I find him out[,] Ile make him[—] he shall remember it as long as he liues. For I'le so bang him, and belabour his sides that he shall neither be able to walke sit or ly a bed.

STR: Then, it seemes, I must stand as long as I live.

CRA: This arch rogue that hath suffer'd all out things at home wch I gaue him in charge to be spoyld. Nay I had made ready some flesh, and fishes. All this he has stole away. And a great Bottle of Aile out of my sellar wch I Kept for my own tooth.

STR: Tis twenty yeares agoe since she had ere a one.

CRA: And this he will liberally drinke of with his ffellow tiplers. [fol. 22v]

ALF: She hath nam'd almost the verry same Cheere I had.

CRA: I haue search't all the taverns, all the Ailhouses, every baudihouse, all Corners and by places, but to no purpose. One may as soone find a Needle in a bottle of hay, as this owle, this night=[/]walking vultur.

str: drinks

STR: Now my Aile or never infuse some courage into me. I had never more need both of thy counsell and assistance; that I may the better endure whatsoever misery falls vpon mee.

CRA: I do'nt see what I should doe in these vnfre=[/]quented places. Ile home again. For now tis almost day. Ile take some other course to correct him for his misdeedes.

STR: Let her goe with a mischiefe, that intends so much to me. But— (*he coughs*) what now— (*coughs again*) I am vndon (*again*)[;] I have betray'd myselfe. (*again*)

CRA: I haue at last found out my youth. The noyse came from this tree. Ho! Come out thou threepeny rascall. Come out thou filching thiefe, thou Ailestealer.

STR: I entreat you[.] O my (*coughs*)[;] he[a]re what I shall say for (*again*) not so much in my defence (*again*) as in my iust excuse (*again*)[.] Wherefore if I haue deserv'd[,][77] (*again*) be you iust (*again*)[;] if I haue not be mercifull[.] (*again*)

CRA: Sayst thou so beast? Thou shall receive a iust punishment from me.

ALF: I must try if I can dissuade this woman. Cease to be [fol. 23]

---

77 That is, "if I have deserved ill-treatment."

so cruell against y^{r} son.

CRA: And who art thou simple fellow who corrects me. A fellow-drunkard of his, and it may be a conspirator in his theevery. Goe about your owne busines. I know what I haue to doe.

Sce: 8.

Denevulphe. Strumbo. Crabula
Alfrede.

What noyse, what disorder is this I heare? What a Stir my wife keepes[,] as if she were pre-[/]paring some tragedy. Strumbo whats the reason thy Mother is so highly incensed against thee?

STR: Because she's a pestilent Creature, and I am born in a Cuntry where trees make war vpon men.—

CRA: Do you answer so of y^{r} Mother[?]

DEN: Pray wife[,] moderate y^{r} passion[;] suspend y^{r} anger till I know all things in their order. Whats the matter strumbo that thou art so threatned?

STR: O ffather. It hapned this night, that without the Knowledge of my mother I went abroad to meete some friends. To this designe I had need of Meat and Aile to strengthen me in my iourney[,] which I confesse I secretly tooke away. Presently I met with this man[,] to me the best of Men, who being almost starv'd with hunger, after I had refresh't with my meat and Aile, thrust this gold into my hand, and freely gaue it me.

DEN: What now haue you, Wife, to say against him?

CRA: Nothing at all. I am now pacify'd now I see the [fol. 23v] Money. O Strumbo my onely Son, thy Mother's deare, and darling, giue me thy money that I may keepe it for thee.

STR: Ile keepe it for you Mother, rather then you for me. For why should you keepe anything for me that am a villaine, a three peny Rascall, a filtching Thiefe, and whats worse an Aile stealer[?]

CRA: My Strumbo, do'nt torment your Mother with new afflictions. Here take you these Rods, and revenge y^{r} selfe. All that I said shall be vnsaid, and all that I haue don vndon. I give you the victory. Give me the Money, My deare Hart, my ioy, my pretty Soule—

STR: Ho! Victory, victory, victory! I haue won ye day. Now

I walke aboue the thundring clouds, and thrust my head amongst the Stars. Tis enough to subdue an enimy; tis noble to shew Clemency to the conquered; wherefore to you, Mother, I deliver my Money, but to be kept for me.

gives her ye gold

CRA: This will buy new Rods to be kept for you. FFarewell; my busines calls me home.

ALF: Old women I see, are not free f[ro]m ye desire of gold.

STR: Now I iudge myselfe worthy of a ffather, or at least of these Rods; who foolishly haue parted with my Money, wch at any time would haue saued my backside from a scowring.

DEN: Put that Care out of y^r Mind. He that contems money shall never want it, and those that too much seeke after it will always be in pursuite.

ALF: This old Man alone caries a generous mind. [fol. 24]

ST: I seeke not after money, nor money after mee because I came to it when least I expected it and lost it without any difficulty at all[;] therefore that wch I did neither seeke to get, nor to loose I must hereafter seeke to regain and to keepe it. My Arguments in forme.

ALF: To wit in Barbara.[78]

DEN: Nor more of this.— Now I desire to know what fortune hath brought this Stranger hither, who hath bin so beneficiall to you.

ALF: The sad event of War hath brought me hither. I am a Souldier enlisted vnder King Alfred's Banners. FFortune hath now made the Danes our Conquerours, and forc't the King to an vnseemly flight; so that the whole Kingdome lyes a prey to mercilesse hands. Gothurnus, every where victorious, reekes with blood, and his insolent ffury spares None. I shelter'd by the wood, and the darknesse of the night, haue with much adoe evaded the pursute of his soldiers[.] Now tis my sole desire to become a companion of y^r tranquility, and change the inquietude of Armes, into the quietnesse of a cuntry life.

DEN: O sad and dolefull fate of a Kingdome
whose ruin's to much[79] to be lamented!
Do's time run away on such vnconstant,

---

[78] "A syllogism in *Barbara* is one in which both the major and minor premisses, and the conclusion, are universal affirmatives: thus, all animals are mortal; all men are animals; . . . all men are mortal"—*OED*, s.v. "barbara."

[79] That is, "too much"; employed here and in other places in MS without distinction for the intensifier "too" as well as the preposition.

Slipery wheeles,[80] that no day can assure
a certain happinesse? Not an hower,[81]
Nor a Moment can promise the durance
of a Life compleatly happy? O the [fol. 24v]
quietnesse of a Poore Cottage, to be
envied even by Kings, lesse happy
then those that laboriously till the earth.
If they knew their owne good. They build not
Edifices, obvious to ev'ry
thunderclap; nor are their towers shaken
by the winds; wherefor (my Guest) embrace that
quiet peace, lodg'd onely vnder the roofe
of a poore Cottage: liue here in safety
till better times apeare. Strumbo driue you
the Hogs where they are vs'd to feed.
STR: Hauing lost my Money I'm now again
become a Swinheard, but I'le be anan[82]
hauing lost my hogs a monied Man.

exeunt

Act: 3

Sce: i

Edward. Eccho.

Elfred! Sister Elfrede speake! Your brother
Calls. How came I thus to loose you? W^{ch} way
alas! Can you direct y^{r} fearefull steps?
FFeare not I am no enimy but a
Brother; ioyn'd to you equally in loue
and Consanguinity. But all my words
vanish into wind. O ffates, too severe!
Is it not cruelty enough to make
me destitute of a ffat[h]er, Kingdome,

---

[80] Though not listed in Tilley, proverbial—"time runs on wheels"; "time flies."
[81] That is, "hour."
[82] Variant of "anon."

of a place of Residence[?]
O my life, more truly ffunerall, still [fol. 25]
aggregated with heapes of miseries!
Here 'midst my enimies, and in a wood
I seeke my Sister, whom the darknesse of
the night, help'd by ye various turnings
of the perfidious way, hath lost from mee.
I haue plac't my Mother in security
And sisters, all but Elfrede, to whom
Ile either be a companion in life
or death. This day shall bring my sister
to me, or by death me to her.
O Nymph inhabiting ye silent vallies;
Thou invisible goddesse of the woods
be propitious and tell me where
Of my lost sister Elfrede I shall heare[.]
Eccho:—Here
Ist in this place then that my sister is[?]
Eccho:—yes
What to regaine her must I vndergoe?
Eccho:—goe
You bid me goe but say not whither.
Eccho:—hither.
How may I yet secure her from all harme?
Eccho:—arme.
Is there any one she's Prisoner to?
Eccho:—two
Tis soe two Danes haue then surpris'd her.
Eccho:—priz'd her.
Prize they her[,] yet detain her 'gainst her will[?] [fol. 25v]
Eccho:—ill
A ffoes Loue soone Chastity divorceth.
Eccho: forceth
O Gods! And doth shee not with griefe abound?
Eccho:—bound.
Can Heau'n with so great wickednes accorde?
Eccho: A Corde.
Bound with a Corde? Why make I these delayes?
Ile either perish with her or vndoe it.
exit
Eccho: doe it.[83]

---

[83] In addition to the conventionality of this kind of scene, which Drury also em-

Sce: 2. ⁜

Osberne.

Ile once again returne from whence I came:
She's fled some other way. Tis strange she thus
should vanish from my sight. But Ile search
all secret Pits, and Concaues[84] of the wood,
to enioy so beautifull a Creature.

exit.

Scen: 3. ⁜

Gormo.

Th' idæa of that virgine which my eyes
iust now beheld, hath left its impression
in my hart. How Beauty was divided
betwixt a blush, and palenesse, caus'd by my
aproach. Whither is my rouing minde
transported? I must pursue, or not liue[;] [fol. 26]
Her embrace shall be my labours reward.

exit

Sce: 4. ⁜

Bragadocia. Pimpo.

Come neerer to me Pimpo.
PIM: I dare not Master.
BRA: Why?
PIM: Because I am not yet weary of my life.
BRA: Whats the matter?
PIM: I desire to stand out of the reach of y^r breath least[85] I should be poysoned to death: for it smels mighty strong of garlicke and onions.

---

ployed in *Reparatus*, note should be taken of Knightley's skill in managing the echo technique while working from the Latin into English.

[84] "A hollow, a cavity"—*OED*, s.v. "concave."

[85] That is, "lest."

BRA: Thou say'st well[;] Ile speake to thee with a gentle breath.

PIM: Doe you see how these trees even with y^e least blast of y^r breath are troubled with y^e palsy: see how the Mountains dance.

BRA: Tis true. Tis my misfortune to bee too strong: and this is the reason why I am not one of the Kings Privy-Counsellors:[86] for if in consul=[/]tation I should be never so little angry I should blow all men neere me into the aire.

PIM: His breath is verry strong indeed, and would infect all the aire about him, so that men would be glad to get as far from it as they could. This is nothing Master. Since you came a warrier into this Cuntry, the Island with y^e[87] [fol. 26v] earthquakes you haue caused is ready to tumble into the sea. What do I speake of an Island? You haue often tost the whole world from on[e] place to another as men do tenis=balls.[88]

BRA: Now lets recount our warlike exploits.

PIM: Those wch you never did. *aside*

BRA: Do'st remember the Names of thos giants this Arme hath made worm's meat of?

PIM: Verry well.

BRA: Lets here some of them.

PIM: FFirst comes into my mind his Name as long as a Cable=rope, wch you kild in the Bombasticothonian[89] ffields. 'Twas if I mistake not fferrierepinomachærofer,[90] and his sirname valorosofustifrangilumbus[.][91] This

---

[86] An explicitly political anachronism.

[87] Catchword for fols. 26–26v.

[88] Seventeenth-century cliché.

[89] Appropriated directly from Drury, this nonsense word suggests the field of bombastic battle. *OED* records that "cothe" as a root meant "sickness, disease" or "pestilence" in the late Middle Ages. Hence, perhaps, the fields of bombastic pestilence.

[90] Another of Drury's nonsense words. The root "mach," suggesting combat, is joined to the prefixes, "ferrier" (=ferryman) and "repine" or "pine." All of these are modified by the suffix "fer," meaning "bearer" or "doer." The general idea is that Bragadocia is being addressed with ironic playfulness and monstrously impressive rhetoric as a repining combatent, a doer of nothing.

[91] The giant's surname, also taken from Drury, suggests fustian (and therefore empty) valor. "Frang" suggests breakable, and when combined with "lumbus," from Latin "loin," connotes a braggart who can be broken at the seat of his masculinity. These bombastic terms redound parodically upon Bragadocia since his exploits are really figments of an overactive imagination. From a theatrical stand-

monster making towards you, you stoutly spit at; which falling vpon his forehead knock't out his braines. The lesser drops wch flew about; vpon the spectators, made them either toot[h]lesse or noselesse.

BRA: Thou hast an excellent memory.

PIM: Tis requisite a lyar should.

BRA: What noyse is that I heare. Pimpo get vp into this tree; clashes of Armour shound[92] in my eares.

PIM: I will if I can.

Pim: gets into ye tree

BRA: What see'st thou?

PIM: O Master, I see a mighty Army advancing this way: I see another. And another yet. Inumerable troops of armed men. Whole groues of Pikes.[93] To[94] tell yee the truth, *aside* I see nothing but one woman. [fol. 27]

BRA: Doe they come this way Pimpo?

PIM: Yes, I tell you hither.

BRA: To this place?

PIM: To this verry place. Are you not afraid Master?

BRA: Not I; I'm not afraid, but onely tremble a little as if a fit of an Ague had iust now ceas'd vpon me.

PIM: O me! O me! Now th[e]y fight. What a slaughter of men do I see? They butcher, and spit on another with their swords. Whomsoever they find in their way they kill without mercy.

Bra: lookes for a place to hide himselfe in

Whats the matter, Master? What do you looke for?

BRA: A place to vntruss a point in. For a suddain loosenesse hath taken me.

runs out

PIM: A suddain feare he should say. He's onely gon to hide himselfe. Now I am onely lord in this place: My master has taken vp his lodging amongst the brambles and bryars. Now Ile privately heare whats the matter with this woman, for she comes as if she were frighted.

---

point, it may be observed that these nonsense words are all easily pronounceable despite their monstrous length.

[92] For modern "sound."

[93] The pikes are imagined as wooden—hence whole groves of them.

[94] Catchword, uncapitalized in MS, for fols. 26v–27.

Sce: 5. ⸫

Elfrede. Pimpo. Bragadocia.

Where shall I repose my wearied limbs?
Or when will my timerous flight find some
Refuge? As well my enimies, as the
Horrour of the dawning day beset round
with caliginous[95] clouds, strikes feare into
my breast. Nor lesse doth the treachery of
the faithlesse night, which alone hath made me [fol. 27v]
destitute of my brother, my sister
and my Mother. And yet I am deny'd
the Curtesy wch death affords. When all
things seeme to conspire my destruction,
and an Army of Miseries assault
One Single virgin. When ev'ry thing
proues treacherous and yet afords not death
the welcome remedy to those that live
in Misery.—

PIM: Sure enough this Prize must not 'scape my Masters hands. Ile goe call him backe, for he hath bin a great while vntrussing.

exit

ELF: To whom shall I become a wretched prey?
Will ye enimy spare me? Hatred swells
his breast. Will he strait with death dispatch me?
Perhaps he'l violate my Chastity
And thus inflict a torment worse then death.
But Ile resist: Alas, I can't. Ile fly:
he'l soone pursue, and force me to his will.

puls out a Knife

Canst thou endure it Elfrede? Rather dy;
Let thy owne hand prevent that grand mischiefe:
Hold. Let piety prevaile. Senslesse wretch,
what dost thou? Wilt thou redeeme
one wickednesse with another and still
accumulate mischifs with new mischifs
more vnexpiable? Relent my Sorrows

throws downe the Knife

and become religous. If Chastity
Can find no refuge; Earth open thy iawes,

---

95 "Misty, dim, murky; obscure, dark"—*OED*, s.v. "caliginous"

I now demand that place of sepulture[96] [fol. 28]
which ere long will be my due. Haue Pitty,
and receive an vndefiled body
into thy pious bosome. O potent
Rector of the Heau'ns either defend

enter Bra: Pim:

Bra: seeing the Knife vpon ye ground starts back.

my body from such wickednesse or else
divorce my soule from so much Misery.

PIM: Master what doe you stand at? Ye prize is before you, take possession of it.

BRA: Is that a sword Pimpo?

PIM: Tis a Knife.

BRA: Put it away. There's no other enemy here besides that may betray vs?

PIM: None at all.

BRA: Are all those Armies vanisht wch you spoke of even now?

PIM: All of them.

BRA: Tis well.

PIM: Goe on therefore. What do you feare?

BRA: I feare nothing. But I looke about me as it becomes a Man that is prudently valliant and valiantly prudent. Lets to her.

they cease[97] vpon her

ELF: O—O— now I perish.

BRA: Pimpo ty her hands, and feete, least she should scratch, or kicke, or run away.

PIM: FFere[98] not. Her nailes are short. Nor hath she any hobnailes[99] in her shoes. Besides how shall we then get her from hence.

BRA: Her fface is handsome enough if it be not painted, she[100] will serue to be one of my Kitchin=Wenches. [fol. 28v]

PIM: Belieue it, this woman is without all fucus[101] or ffallacy: not because she weepes for this is com̃on to all

---

96 "Interment, burial"—*OED*, s.v. "sepulture."

97 Obsolete form of "seize"—*OED* s.v. "cease."

98 Variant of "fear."

99 "A nail with a massive head and short tang, used for protecting the soles of heavy boots and shoes"—*OED*, s.v. "hobnail."

100 Catchword for fols. 28–28v.

101 "Paint or cosmetic for beautifying the skin; a wash or colouring for the face"—*OED*, s.v. "fucus."

women, but because she is silent.

Sce: 6.

Osberne. Gormo. Bragadocia.
Pimpo. Elfrede.

At length I see the fface wch hath enflam'd me.
GOR: I see those eyes from whence I borrow life.
osb: gor: not seeing one another
OSB: She's fallen into a souldiers hands.
GOR: She's become a pray[102] to a proud boaster.
OSB: He shall not take her hence away and liue.
GOR: He shall resigne her vp to me or dye.
BRA: Now Pimpo bring her after me in state ffor now I'le goe new triumphs to create.[103]
meets gor: and runs back:
PIM: What ailes you Master? Why doe you run away? Whats the matter?
BRA: Doe you aske? The Stars fall, the heauens are ready to overwhelme me. I must be gon.
PIM: 'S foot, what ist you run from?
BRA: The world totters. Neverthelesse I do'nt run but I walke a great pace.
GOR: Deliver vp the virgine. She is Mine.
OSB: She's neither his nor yours, but mine alone.
GOR: Osberne!
OSB: Gormo!
GOR: What brought you hither?
OSB: My lust.
GOR: And me my loue.
OSB: This virgin's Mine. [fol. 29]
GOR: I deny't.
OSB: Our showrds[104] shall end the dispute.
GOR: They shall. Death or she, shall be my prize.
PIM: Defer y^r ffight, till a third Combatant, my master, puts in his claime—What are you yet silent? FFright 'em with the thunder of y^r words. Whilst two dogs fight the bones may come to y^r share.

---

[102] That is, "prey."

[103] The awkward syntax of the second line issues from the desire to make the rhyme.

[104] Obsolete form of "swords."

BRA: Ile try. Although I scarse thinke this girle worth so much, as to incense my implacable Anger. Or that I should earthquake the world: and reduce it to its antique Chaos, for one wenches sake; Or that I should disarme Joue himselfe of his thunderbolts; enthrone my selfe in the Chaine of Divinity; force the Gods into exile; breake Mars's legs; and Knock out Hercules's teeth; make Vulcane Limp with both legs; pull of Jupiter's eares, Saturns beard; Apollo's lockes; Juno's Nose, Scratch out Venus's eyes; yet before this prize shall be taken from me, I'le let loose the raines of my ffury.[105]

OSB: Dost arme thy selfe?

GOR: Dos't draw thy sword?

OSB: Thou trumpeter of thy owne ffame.

GOR: Detractor of anothers.

OSB: Thou ffearefull—

GOR: Coward.

OSB: Cockscombe.

GOR: Asse.

PIM: I believe, of an Asse, hee'l strait be meta=[/] morphis'd [fol. 29v] into lesse then a Mouse. Master, if you'l take my counsell, either ffight or r[u]n away.

BRA: O Pimpo. Thou know'st I am verry valliant, I am also verry patient. Ile neither run away nor fight, but Ile be gon, and acquaint the King with the whole busines; hee'l give me thankes that I forbore to take my iust revenge, vpon his Brother and Kinsman. But stand thou at a distance, that I may strike 'em dead with one word, wch I vse to shake Cuntry's with[;] tis the thunder and light'ning of my Name[—]he[a]re it and tremble for now I pronounce it: Polemobombardifragosogigantomiomacho=[/] pomponides.[106]

runs out

---

[105] Fine example of Drury's maximizing the uses of his stock characters. Here the *miles gloriosus* is also the pedant.

[106] More of Drury's philological playfulness. Bragadocia is again defined mock-heroically—this time as a bellicose, self-centered, pompous hurler of words. "Polem" in Greek means to wage war or signifies one who wages war (a warrior). The prefix also suggests "polemicist"—hence, parodically, a "word-warrior" who "bombards" his opponents. If "fragoso" is derived from "fragor," it means "A loud harsh noise, a crash, din." The term "giganto" is self-explanatory, and "mio," meaning "my" or "mine," emphasizes the egoism of the speaker, while "macho-pomponides" suggests a mechanical (or perhaps machinating) pomposity. See *OED*, s.v. "Polemist," "Fragor," "Machinate."

PIM: This Name reaches to the Antipodes, where it
demolishes whole Kingdomes. Thus my Master
vanquisheth his enemies with the verry sound of his
Name, and being Conquerour runs away. Ile withdraw a
little and see what passes.
OSB: Gormo, wee are now alone, if thy Courage
serves, lo, nows the time: I stand thy enimy
Or thy ffriend; thy friend if thou resigne
This virgin; thy enimy if thou refuse.
GOR: Gormo neither feares Osbern as an
Enimy, nor contemns him, as a ffriend.
Thy Claime to her makes thee equally
an enemy vnto me and a ffriend.
OSB: Do'st then vnsheath thy sword.
GOR: Against thy Breast.
ELF: Suspend y^{r} Rage; and heare an vnfortunate [fol. 30]
virgine speake before you embrew[107] y^{r} hands
in each others blood. But what shall I say?
How shall I parly with two Enimies,
two Louers, and in this so much the more
to be hated by me. For if they were
Not Louers, I should then be exempted
from the horrour of Loues evell effects:
If they were onely enimies, that feare
would vanish; Death's the worst an enimy
Can inflict; but from a louer I feare
a worser Mischiefe. The vnrepared
losse of virginity is more killing
then death itselfe; and to this, more precious
then life, louers are more inimicall
then enimies. Are you therefore Louers
or Enimies to me? If enimies,
why haue y^{r} hands thus long spared my life?
If Louers, why do you seeke after blood?
You know, as louers to me you'r more
my enimies; 'twould be much better to be
louers to y^{r} selves and enimies to me[.]
Let y^{r} quarrell dy in my death.
Let this beauty (if any) be destroy'd,
the incentiue wch hath animated
Louers, but my enimies, to assume

[107] That is, "embrue" or "imbrue."

their armes, design'd against each others breast:
I am th'occasion of your quarrell,
w^{ch}, if you end my life, will likewise haue [fol. 30v]
and end. Lo, I kneele to you; and to you
become a supplicant; if a tygre
was not y^{r} Nurse; if a fierce lyonesse
gaue you not sucke, haue pitty on y^{r} selues
and, if you afford me death, on me too.
OSB: What doe we do? Shall we dispatch this Lette[108]
t'our Combat; and terminate our quarrell,
or else go on with our incepted[109] worke?
GOR: Sure enough wee'l on: and yet I could scarse
abstain from teares. But tis effeminate
to be mou'd at ye complaints of a woman.
OSB: That we may with a more free arme
attend our businesse, wee'l binde ye virgine
to a tree least she make an escape.
GOR: Contented. Let her be bound.

they binde her to a tree.

OSB: Now to y^{r} sword.
GOR: Begin.

they fight and breathe awhile

Sce: 7.

Edward, Osberne. Gormo.
Elfrede.

What Clashing of Armes within this vally
retorts a sound from the redoubled blows
And calls me hither[?] Whats this? Behold,
some cruell hand hath bound my Sister
to a tree. This, I easily conclude,
is the cause hat[h] provok't this single fight,
That the Conquerour may enioy the Prize. [fol. 31]
'Twas this, the Eccho ffrom a solitary
recesse pronounc'd to me. What shall I do?
Can I so young, myselfe encounter two?
Shall I an vnexperienced youth

---

108 A "let" or "lett(e)" is an obstruction or hindrance, as in a net-cord or "let ball" in tennis. See *OED*, s.v. "let."

109 "To undertake; to begin, commence, enter upon"—*OED*, s.v. "incept."

alone attaque two expert Captaines?
Tis better, stay till the vncertain chaine
of victory crownes one. His shall be the
breast my sword shall point at: this advantage
will more surely worke my sisters ffreedome.
OSB: Yealld to me at length the prize we fight for.
GOR: Ile sooner yeeld my life; or take thine.

they fight
Gormo falls

OSB: I came not of without bloud, my conquest
hath cost me wonds, and ye death of a friend.
But at last she's ffallen into my hands.
EDW: Thou ly'st. She is fallen into my hands.
Hold Monster. Thou dy'st if thou touch her.
OSB: What boy art thou, who thus insults ore me?
EDW: I'm cald Edward: son of a king, and brother
to this Virgine. And an enimy to thee.
ELF: Heau'n I see relieues the miserable.
OSB: The long look't for, and much desired day
wherein I'le extirpate the progeny
of thy ffather comes of its owne accord.
My potent Arme shall eradicate with
one blow that hatefull generation.
EDW: Spare now yr words, tis time you fall to deeds.
The insulting enimy is fallen

they fight
Osb: falls

How the ponderous Bulke of his expiring [fol. 31v]
Body indents the earth. O sweet sister!
ELF: O Brother, more welcome to me then life!

embraces her.
and vnbinds her.

EDW: Lets now be gon, our foes are ev'ry where.

exeunt
osb: rises

OSB: Thou shalt not thus come of a Conqueror.
My arme shall yet make death attend its stroak.
What now? My leggs faile me. My eyes are mask'd
with night, my vitall breath desists to doe
its office. All my ioynts are stupify'd
as if arrested by approaching death.
Now I know not where I am[,] Or whither.

falls down

FFalling. Gormo I come to thee, I dye
A Companion of thy death who am ye Cause.

GOR: Oh— oh—
OSB: Lets be conioyn'd in death
Thô life seperated vs. O Cruell
Horrour oth' Minde! O neverending sleepe!

Sce: 8.

Pimpo.

Art awake Pimpo? Or dos't thou sleepe with thy eyes open? If I am awake I'm sure those two are not. For they sleepe faster then if they should snort and snore. If I sleepe then they are awake; and the dead liue. I had rather be asleepe then be thus awake. I commend my Master who chose rather to loose his Prize and all his great words too, then his life by fighting. Now I must see whether the dead haue any money[110] to lend those that are [fol. 32] liuing: for amongst the liuing money is but dead, being buried in the Chests of rich Men, so that it neuer sees light: afterwards the owners being dead, it liues again, as it now falls out. Now Ile to the King, and relate the whole businesse.

exit

Sce: 9.

Neothus. Osberne. Gormo.

My Minde presages some strang accident,
which makes me leaue my Cell[,] and thus alone
like an errant[111] wander ye silent woods
whither fortune or providence directs.
What doe I see? Behold two dead bodies
lying vpon the ground: their ffaces beare
death's horrid picture wch life eraseth.
O the torrent of Rage drowning itselfe.
Anger can't haue more cruell enimies

[110] Catchword for fols. 31v–32.
[111] As a noun, an "errant" is a rover or one who travels.

then itselfe: though Scithia[112] should be searcht,
Or that Icy land wch lyes congeal'd
vnder the ffreezing North it cannot find
A salvage beast more rabid then itselfe.
But why doe I delay? Evells require
a Remidy and not words. Ile try if
my med'cines can retrieue their flying soules.
Charity this much obliges, to help
the miserable, thô our enimies.

goes to ye Corps

Life hath not yet quite left this Corps: nor this.
A faint breath comes from them both. Eeven as [fol. 32v]
A Sparke lyes buried in the ashes
ready to disapeare. So their soules remaine
fomenting still that sparke of life, almost
extinguish't by their wonds. This Balsome w^ch^
I allwayes carry with me for pious
vses, when aply'd will ease their wonded
Bodies, and force their hou'ring soules returne

applyes his balsome

to ev'ry Member.[113] Thou great Arbitour
of the world, giue health to their soules and to
their bodies life. See[!] They stir[,] and begin
to send forth groaning sighs: their couler apeares.
Their senses reassume their proper Orgains.

GOR: Where am I? What splendor invests my eyes?
OSB: What Cuntry, in what part oth' world am I?
GOR: Doe I liue again?
OSB: Is life return'd?
GOR: Am not I yet sunke to the Infernall Lake?
OSB: Is not my conscious Soule yet suffocated
with stygian horridnesse?
GOR: What torments was I ready to endure?
OSB: What terrours of death haue I avoyded?
GOR: How immense is the divine Goodnesse?
OSB: How terrifying is the Celestiall maiesty?
GOR: O Let me ever bewale
the wicked actions of my misspent life.

---

112 Sythia. Loosely associated with the East and with the central Asian tribes of Indo-European origin; geographically with eastern Turkey and north-western Iran. See *OCD* (968).

113 The balsam Neothus applies to bodies virtually dead prompts the soul to return to every limb or member of the body.

OSB: O that a time for teares might be granted.
NEO: It shall. Let griefe absterse[114] y^{r} former sins;
Christ by his death hath bestow'd life on you[;]
offer that same life to him: by his own wounds. [fol. 33]
He hath animated y^{r} bodies.
Dedicate y^{r} soules and bodies to so
bountifull a Lord. What neede I say more?
Liue worshipers of Christ whose eternall
Deity, you haue hitherto deny'd
with obstinate impieties.
OSB: I acknowledge ye Deity of Christ[.]
GOR: I adore it.

musicke as from heaun

NEO: Reioice yee celestiall Inhabitants.
What's this I heare? What sweet harmony sounds
to my eares? All the heau'nly choristers
Crowne this happy day with ioy, and extoll
their Master so mercifull to Mortalls.
Tis now requisite you should giue some rest
to y^{r} feeble Bodies. Let my shoulders
support y^{r} armes[;] Ile be y^{r} guide to shew
the way; and ere long ye author of y^{r} health.
Thus my Redeemers sheepe that goe astray
I carry home and set them in their way.

exeunt

Sce: 10.

Gothurnus. Bragadocia.
Pipero. Titmus, Soldiers.

Shall then the beauty of a girle retarde
our glory? And the alluring deceit
of a flattering fface thus greedily
Steale away the laurell from ye victour? [fol. 33v]
Was it this that provok'd my Captaines to
an inconsiderate Combat? Madnese!
I thinke we are Amorists not Enimies.
We haue not gloriously su[b]iugated
A Kingdome; but shamefully submitted

[114] "To wipe away; to wipe clean, to cleanse"—*OED*, s.v. "absterge."

to a fœminine yoke: we are become
Captiues to ye proud lookes of a woman,
to whose triumphs we haue debas't ourselves.
Nature, art thou not assham'd of Mankind?
Acknowledge now this grand errour in thy
workmanship, to haue created Men and
made the[m] subiect to womens tyrannies.

Sce: 11. ≠

Pimpo. Gothurnus. etc.

Great King: I bring the message of sad newes:
its relation I tremble to rehearse.
GOTH: Speake, if it is concerning my Brother;
what was the event of their femele Combat?[115]
PIM: After a mutuall ffury had incens'd
their firy spirits to spill each others
blood: they bound the virgin to a tree. I,
secretly lying hid in the adiacent
wood, was a spectator of all that past.
Gormo fell by Osberns hand; who 'scap't not
without wounds[,] when a young Man comes into
the place, calls Osbern to his Armes againe,
Kills him, frees his sister being (as he said) [fol. 34]
King Alfredes son, and fly's away with her.
GOTH: Infernall Night for ever cloud this day
with horrid darknesse! Thou fatall owle be
silent: shall I then nere see my Captaines
but soe, without their breath? Shall I, thus crown'd
with Roses and laurells climbe Englands throne
And thus behold my triumphs, elated,
in a splendid Chariot? O Gods!
I call ye cruell; say you'r impotent;
Nay more that ye are not at all. Appeare
yee ffuries[;] my breast yealds itselfe alone
to y^r scourges: Ætna[116] that vomets vp
sulphureous flames give place: I am consum'd.
with a more violent ffire; I must

---

[115] Not "womanish" combat but combat *over* a woman ("female").
[116] Ætna, located in Sicily, is Europe's highest active volcano.

lament my brother osbern's death: O No,
A funerall howle must rather bewale him;
till the verry abisses of darknesse
Restore me the loved Name of Osberne;
but his Name? That, it seemes is all that's left
of my brother, but he himselfe never
to apeare before my eyes, being detain'd
in th' infernall concaues of the earth
and shut from my sight by th' adamantine
dores of Pluto's pallace: shut from my sight?
This sword shall hew a passage to him,
Ile ransacke Death's Teritories: and make-
Styx, and Cocitus, wch haue swallowed
him vp, vomet out my Osberne.

Sce: 12. ⫽ [fol. 34v]

Second Messenger. Gothurnus. etc.

My Liege, in Order to y^r^ commands we went
to the verry place where the Combat was[,] y^t^
we might bring you their Bodies either
dead or alive: But, we know not by whose
hands or by what deceit, their dead bodies
are remou'd from the place. The earth was
dyed with purple tinctures of bloud, wch by
the print of their bodies made vs easily
distinguish, that was the place they fell in.
GOTH: Stop thy vnlucky throat; or Ile teare thy
tongue from betwixt thy iawes. Purposely you
bawle this newes into my eares; Now Gormo
and my Brother ready arm'd claime a Virgine;
Now my Brother is victorious over Gormo;
Now my Brother lyes subdued by ye Armes
of a hated Enimy. And Now you
tell me my Brothers Corps and Gormo's too
are conveighed away. And ly vnburied
perhaps a food for salvage Animalls.
Or what's far worse possest by th' Enimy.

Sce: 13.

Third Messenger. Gothurnus. etc.

Haldene, Hingar, and Hubba, three Kings neere ally'd to you, both by blood and ffriendship, brought their auxiliary fforces for y^r interest but being vanquisht in a fight with ye Britans, haue lost both their liues and all their Artilery.

Sce: 14. # [fol. 35]

ffourth Messenger. Gothurnus. etc.

Great King—
GOTH: Thou screetching Raven!
strikes him downe.
Will ye all thus be Croaking in my eares?
draws his sword vpon his attendants
Learn at y^r perills sometimes to hold y^r peace.
Bra: falls down and creeps into ye bryars.
Doe you run? Y^e shall scarse outrun my Rage.
O too too patient in my Anger!
Call down ye Gods with an imperious voice;
and Marshall that treacherous, impious Band
against me; like Atlas Ile encounter all.
Doe's the supernall Crew then, envy me?
Perhaps they were affraid least after earth
their Heaven should next become due to my
vncontroled triumphs. So 'twas. Ile climbe
Heav'ns lucide spheare and dislocate the stars;
Nor shall the Sun afford ye world his light;
Nor ye Moone lend any brightnesse to th' earth:
Joue shall not find within the Orbs a seat
secure, till Osbern's death he expiate.
exit

Sce: 15.

Pimpo. Bragadocia.

FFor certaine our King's either mad, or I dreame. But if one that's affraid be mad, then I'm sure I was. For I was horribly affraid, that I should haue bin lost into the

Clowds as lycas[117] was by Hercules; and saluted the skyes wch my brains dasht out. From[118] whence I must haue bin [fol. 35v] forc't to take the earth in my way to hell, to find out some Esculapious[119] to cure mee. 'Tis an old saying that fortune favours the couragious; I haue now learn't that it also favours the ffearefull. For by my feare, I haue run into a pit verry beneficiall to me, for in it I found these Cloaths, wch as you see are verry sumptuous; and regall too, for if I mistake not, I saw King Alfrede in these Robes at the beginning of the fight. I guesse the whole story to be thus: After Alfrede had lost ye day, tis likely he chang'd his cloath's, that his flight might be the securer. For in running away it often falls out even amongst Kings, that they haue more care of their liues then of their Cloaths. Hauing now this fit occasion I designe a pretty passage. But first I must call hither my Master. Ho! Master! Nothing of this great Colossus[120] appeares but his feete; if y^{e} sky should chance now to fall vpon his heeles, hee would soone kicke it backe into its proper spheare. My Master is not now afraid, he onely providently measures how much of the Earth he can em=[/]brace in his Armes. Come forth Master. Now my Master dares not heare for his eares. I must release him from these straits.

Pim: pulls him out by y^{e} heeles.

BRA: Quarter, quarter! Who are you? Are you Pimpo or y^{e} ghost of Pimpo? Cam'st thou hither from y^{e} supernall or infernall habitations?

PIM: Y^{r} Magnanimity makes me that I am neither at the one nor the other; those in the infernall Residences[121] are affraid [fol. 36] least you should by force ransome me from them, and those in the supernall feare as much least in freeing me you should vsurpe heau'n to y^{r} selfe. But pray Master what did you doe here? I belieue you did not hide y^{r} selfe.

---

[117] King Lycus, tyrant and rival of Hercules who sought to marry Megara in Seneca's *Hercules Furens*. After hearing of Lycus's outrages, Hercules slew him, but the blood upon his hands gradually brought the hero to madness.

[118] Catchword, uncapitalized in MS, for fols. 35–35v.

[119] That is, "Aesculapius," Latinized form of Asclepius, Greek hero and god of healing.

[120] Like a great statue, but carrying the implication, as in Chapman's *Bussy D'Ambois*, I.i.5–10 [Nicholas Brooke, ed. (London: Methuen, 1964)], that the greatness is empty.

[121] Catchword, uncapitalized in MS, for fols. 35v–36.

BRA: I onely laid my eare to the ground, to heare what the discourse of me is amongst ye Antipodes. If you had not come hither when you did, I had gon directly to hell, and fetch't backe the Kings Brother[,] or at least to haue beaten Cerberus[122] ye threeheaded Porter. But what hast thou here?

PIM: Give attention vnto me; and Ile tell you what 'tis, and how much it availes vs. These are the Robes of King Alfrede wch after his defeat he had hid. I verry oportunely haue found them[,] and would haue you put them on with all expedition.

BRA: And what then?

PIM: Haue patience and Ile tell you. Hauing put them on, goe to our King.

BRA: Goe on.

PIM: Tell him you haue Kild Alfrede.

BRA: Well.

PIM: And then chalenge the thousand pounds, which he promis'd for y^{r} reward.

BRA: Exellent. But is not this a lye?

PIM: As if you nere told a lye before.

BRA: But will he belieue me? [fol. 36v]

PIM: Not[123] I although you should sweare. *aside* The Cloaths will speake for you.

BRA: But what if it should fall out otherwise, and it should be proued that Alfrede is not Kild?

PIM: The Money will bee in y^{r} Custody; you may goe where you will.

BRA: Thou sayst verry well. Put them on me.

Pim: helps him to put'em on

Now I am [a] King[,] ev'ry inch of me.[124] I want nothing but a Crowne.

PIM: A Cockscombe would fit his head excellently well.

BRA: I'm now a King but in this outward weede
A thousand Pound will make me so indeede.

ex:

---

[122] Three-headed dog guarding the portals of Hades.

[123] Catchwords for fols. 36–36v.

[124] Intriguing inasmuch as the line echoes Lear's famous ejaculation, "ev'ry inch a king!" (4.6.107).

Act: 4:

Sce: i.

Alfrede. Adelvolde.

Hauing left my Mother at home, to wit,
the house of Denevulphe, I am now
accompanied onely with Adelvolde,
going to Neothus a Man verry
eminent for sanctity and of a
neere Relation to myselfe: for whom
I haue a pious regard, beeing a
Priest officiating at ye holly[125]
Altar of the immortall Deity.
And one much venerated for his Name
And function. He hath often foretold
things wch haue allready happened
And those Miseries wch I now endure:
Now disguised with this habite of a [fol. 37]
Common souldier, Ile desire to know
what event will period these Misfortunes.
See, he comes forth. Childe retire, and keepe
thy selfe vndiscovered in this wood.

Adl: withdraws

Sce: 2.

Neothus. Alfrede. Adelvolde.

What is the life of Man still hurl'd away
On swif't wheeles? What do's a day, or a yeare
Availe vs? Who's so voide of Sense, to track
the footsteps of the Winde[,] or so slender=
witted, to expect an impression
from a full saild Ship promiscuously
Cutting the reciprocated waters
with a reversing waue?[126] Life renders
No other account of all that time which

---

[125] Variant of holy.

[126] A knotty image: who can expect a full-sailed ship to create a wake when the (reversing) waves it cuts through obliterates the impression.

still passes away. But It was; it is;
and Shall bee; that wch Was is vanished
like smoake into the aire; that wch Shall bee
beguiles vs with vncertaine hopes of Good;
And that which is, wee loose, whilst we haue it,
Or spend it ill. Or else becomes absent
by being present. If life be Nothing,
who can be Miserable? Since that, life
niether makes vs happy, nor ye contrary;
Tis ye Minde, Christens that life wretched, w^{ch}
Impatiently tollerates its evells;
And that happy wch well employs its good.
ALF: How much that document confutes my errour? [fol. 37v]
Who call[s] that life Miserable which is
clog'd with adversity, and that happy
wch is opulent with prosperity.
NEO: Tis a generous Minde that can endure
miseries with an vnmou'd comportment;
and Insolent, that's inhanc'd with riches:
vertue appeares more in adverse storms,
then when the prosperous gal[e]s of fortune
swell the Minde.
ALF: As a gloomy day at the Aspect of
the Sunne vncloudes its dusky countenance
as if painted with a suddain tincture
of light, and powdered with golden Rayes:
Soe I with the eloquence of his voice
am corroborated with a new strength
of Minde; and my breast lik[e] an adamant
is impregnable to all Miserie:
Ile goe to him. If you are at leasure
to speake some Comfort to the Afflicted
doe it now.
NEO: I will. But first vnmaske y^{r} selfe, and take
y^{r} true and proper Name of King Alfrede.
And call y^{r} son. D'you seeme to wonder?
Thô you may cousen[127] me, you can't deceive
the Omniscient Deity of God.
ALF: This homely dresse wch I weare makes me blush.
NEO: Are you yet proud, hauing lost y^{r} Kingdom?
ALF: A King allways should apeare in splendor.

---

[127] Meaning, "deceive or fool."

NEO: Yet the King of Kings was poorely cloath'd[,] [fol. 38]
and refusing princely Pallaces
chose to liue obscurely in a Cottage.
ALF: He liu'd vnknown to th' World.
NEO: But dying he was Known to th' world; and gaue
vs true examples that life ought not
to faint at evells. What if God hath decree'd
the los[s]e for ever of y^{r} Kingdome?
ALF: O how miserable would my life bee?
What afflictions should I vnhappily
vndergoe? The Barbarous enimy
will adulterate my deare wife before
my fface; and in revenge of me, will cause
my daughters to be contaminated
by libidinous Rapes, murther my Sons,
and afflict me with miseries, torments,
And losse of all; and what is greater yet,
perhaps will spare my life.
ADEL: Griefe I hope will kill me before these sad
Disasters happen.
NEO: O blind Ignorance of Men! Vnbrid'led
ffury of the Minde offending against
itselfe and God[!] You esteeme y^{r} selfe then
miserable when you suffer Evells,
I thought you had bin miserable when
you had committed them. Whilst paine doth
aggrevate the Sense, ye fault's forgotten.
You abhorre the event of Misery;
The Cause alas! is most to be feared; [fol. 38v]
When Potent with an awfull hand you held
Great Britan's Scepter, you ought not to haue
bin insolent with too much felicity;
nor should you haue bin facile to Anger,
prone to punishment, nor proudly rul'd
that flock, wch god comĩtted to y^{r} Charge
on better conditions; nor deny'd
Assistance to the poorest of y^{r} Creatures;
Nor y^{r} Care to Widdows, nor y^{r} Mercy
To the guilty, nor your Riches to y^{e}
Indigent; nor y^{r} loue to y^{r} Subiects;
Nor y^{r} Devotions and feare to God:
Nor precipitately to haue indulg'd
y^{r} Mind to the wantonnesse of pleasures:
God Created you a king, and you make

y^{r} selfe a Tyrant; wretched, Nobody.
ALF: At length I owne ye errours of my life[;]
I now acknowledge Heau'ns patience,
and my owne wickednesse. Wherefore I aske
not a period to my punishment:
I, the onely Author will expiate
those offenses I haue perpetrated;
they are my Sins, let ye hand of god draw
me to satisfaction: he that is wont
to be mercifull to all; let him throw
all his iustice on me alone; but I
Craue, that hand of Anger may be to me
A healing one. Yet let these be preserv'd[;]
they haue merited nothing; let my Cuntry,
Let my Poeple escape this heavy scourge: [fol. 39]

Kneeles

Behold, I humbly, prostrate at y^{r} feete,
Resigne the Name of King, and my Kingdome
now violated with my offences
I give to Heau'n from whence I receiv'd it.
What ist I give since I haue nothing left
to give? What improvidently I haue lost,
Alas! I cannot be a Doner of.
But I give the Name; that's forfeited too,
by raigning vitiously. What shall I doe[?]
Heau'n demands that Kingdome wch I haue not
And the Name of King, wch I haue also lost.
But whatsoever of my selfe is left
I give, that God may distinguish betwixt
Man wch he created in me, and those
ffoule, wicked deeds wch hee's no author of.
ADEL: My ffathers teares call mine to attend them.
NEO: Rise, God hath beheld y^{r} sorrows with a
Compationate[128] looke; he hath disper'ct
the Clouds of his Anger, and pardon sits
character'd on his indulgent Countenance.
His voice speakes Mercy; and promises far
greater Kingdoms then those y^{e} Danes possesse.
Wherefore returne with ioy from whence you came
And liue gratefull to God and mindfull of me.

exit

---

[128] That is, "compassionate."

ALF: Lets goe. I want expressions to declare
the satisfaction wch my Mind doth beare.

exeunt

Sce: 3. # [fol. 39v]

S$^{t.}$ Cuthbert.

I haue now assum'd this Beggars habite.
whereby, trying the charitable hand
of King Alfred I may exhibite him
a Patern to the world, and a pious
example to future generations;
Hee's now return'd from Neothus, and strait
will bring Edward and Elfrede home wth him,
wch I haue preserv'd from the menacing
dangers of enimies, and brought them safe
to th' path wch will leade them to their ffather.
Ile remaine silent and vndiscover'd
in this Place, and will take a time when hee
himselfe shall want y^{t} Almes wch I will begge.
Loe, Osberga and her landlord, come forth.

Sce: 4.

Denevulphe. Osberga.

My Guest, I much desire to know what sadnesse
thus disturbs you; tis no triviall Matter
wch disquiets y^{r} breast with assiduall
pensivenesse, and oft fetches groaning sighs
from ye bottome of y^{r} hart: Cease at length
to let loose ye raines of griefe; and declare
what tis that wounds you[.] Cou[n]sell oftentimes
extenuates great Evells.
OSB: My sorrows
are beyond the Cure of Counsell, nor can
they be leniated[129] by any words; [fol. 40]
for y^{t} wch god hath don cannot find

[129] Literally, made more lenient—palliated, attenuated.

a Remedy but from ye same hand.
DEN: The hand of god wch wounds and y^{t} wch cures
is equally to be tollerated
with an obsequious resignement.
OSB: I bewaile the comõn damage of you,
of myselfe, and of every one.
DEN: Tis a common way to cure miseries,
to reflect that god inflicted them.
OSB: Gods Anger Knows no measure, when he
punisheth our Crimes.
DEN: Nor is his Mercy limited.
But behold, y^{r} Son's retur[n]'d, and beares
I see, a pleasant countenance being
accompanied with new associates.

Sce: 5.

Alfrede, Osberga. Edward.
Elfrede. Adelvolde. Dene[v]ulphe.

I am dubious wch more to congratulate,
my Owne or my Childerns wellcome.
This I'm Certain, that nobody can give
Condigne Prayses to God who hath preserv'd
them safe from all their Enimies.
OSB: This Company will give our sorows some
abatement: but this Comfort ere long will
be taken from vs.
ALF: My hope promises a better ffortune[.]
OSB: But my feare suggests a worse. [fol. 40v]
ALF: Haue Confidence.
OSB: He that expects a Mischiefe knows better
how to endure it.
ALF: But that wch we expect
we endure with greter[130] reluctancy;
for Paine is nourisht by anticipation.
ELF: Nere cease to hope, for God to one that hopes
assuredly will send reliefe.
ADEL: Deare Grand Mother refraine ye tyde of griefe,
an vnexpected day of ioy will Come.

[130] Obsolete variant of "greater."

OSB: 'Twere vaine and foolish, to grive[131] for myselfe,
but my disquiets depend on Many;
the danger of y^{r} safety disturbs me,
the irreparable losses of my
dying Cuntry afflicts me. I prize not
my life now so much as to run from death.
ALF: That poore Man expects me, Ile goe to him.

Sce: 6.

$S^{t.}$ Cuthbert. Alfrede. Osberga.
Edward. Elfrede. Adelvold: Denvulphe.

ffor Christs sake, bestow some ffood vpon one
thats ready to starve for cruell hunger.
ALF: Pray, Mother, if there by any bread left
bring it out of our storehouse, that I may
give it to this poore Man: tis a Crime
exit osb
to deny any thing ask'd for Christs sake.
I Know what misery is, and must learne
by my own example, to relieue [fol. 41]
the afflicted, least ye heav'nly Doner
enter osb: with a loafe
should deny my owne supplications.
OSB: I find but one onely loafe to be left
of all our provisions, with wch you must
relieue y^{r} owne and y^{r} Children's hunger.
ALF: This alone then is left of all my wealth
to maintaine my ffamily. However
Ile haue it divided, that both his want
and mine may somewhat be satisfyed.
The greatest neede shall haue the greatest share;
Wherefore take you this halfe loafe for y^{r} selfe.
He that five thousand fed and with five loaues
satisfyed the hunger of them all;
will provide for me, my Children, and for all.
$S^{T.}$ CUTH: Let his bounty repay this Curtesy.
ALF: Denevulphe, my honest landlord, you see
Our Number is encreast[;] do you provide

---

[131] Obsolete form of "grieve."

Meat as you can; our safety lyes in you.
DEN: Ile doe my endeavour, thô this cloudy weather be not favorable for fishing. Ile try both the Rivers and fishponds.

Sce: 7.

Denevulphe. Strumbo. Crabula
Alfrede. etc.

enter Str:

Ho! Strumbo!
STR: What would you haue ffather? Oh. Oh!
DEN: What ailes you? Come bring ye nets after me.
STR: Oh! [fol. 41v]
DEN: We must both of vs goe worke.
STRO: Oh! Oh!
DEN: Whats ye Matter with thee?
STR:I am sicke all over me, and in every part of me, first my Head akes[132]as if my braines would fly out, my stomach broyles, and belches forth vnsavery smells; my belly twinges me with griping[133] pangs a Cough almost choakes me, and a loosenesse hath almost fretted out my bowells. What can I say more? I am not so much sick as sicknesse itselfe.
DEN: Wheres my wife? Ho! Crabula! Crabula!

enter Cra:

CRA: What a mischiefe's the matter wth you husband? What a noise is here as if you were mad? I thinke ye house is turn'd into an ailehouse.
DEN: Haue a Care of y^{r} Son, who is verry sicke, whilst I goe out a fishing for privision for my guests.
CRA: What guests? What to doe a fishing? With a vengence! Whats their businesse here who sent for 'em? Let 'em be gon from hence with a pox to 'em, they must eat y^{r} meat whilst you y^{r} selfe are hungry at y^{r} owne house.
DEN: Good wife be not in such a Rage; good words will much better become you. Ile now be gon; you in the mean time carry y^{r} selfe civilly.

---

[132] "Earlier and better spelling of ACHE"—*OED*, s.v. "ake"

[133] Strumbo claims to have pangs that clench, squeeze, or "grip" his belly. See *OED*, s.v. "griping."

ALF: Let's goe in and rest ourseleues

exeunt
all but str: Cra:

Sce: 8. # [fol. 42]

Crabula. Strumbo.

What's ye Matter with thee Strumbo?
STR: Oh! Pray hold me.
CRA: What ailes thee?
STR: Doomsday is come. My legs faile me.
CRA: How pale he grows of a suddain; woe is mee! Strumbo is falling; hee's in a sownd. What shall I doe? Strumbo, my strumbo revive alittle.
STR: Oh! Oh!
CRA: I can scarse hold him vp; he is as heavy as lead. Raise thyselfe a little.

Str: in y^e mean time puts his hand
into her pocket and takes out her purse

STR: Oh!
CRA: A little more. Yet againe.— Take this stoole and sit downe a while. Will you haue any Aqua=vitæ?
STR: No, No; I am now some thing better.
CRA: Will you haue a bit of gingerbread wch lyes in the bottome of my purse?
STR: O No. Pray Mother let it alone. I hate ginger=[/]bread; nor can looke vpon it without falling into a sownd.
CRA: Wilt thou haue money then, to buy thee something?
STR: I beseech you Mother torment me not, if you haue any care of my health. Money? I had rather see y^e Divell now then Money. If you loue me take away y^r hand; I abhorre y^e very sight of the purse.
CRA: Tis a strange sicknesse wch makes money to be hated, I [fol. 42v] am[134] affraid tis mortall; for if I were halfe dead and should see Money I should quicly[135] recover.
STR: Oh!— that verry word hath almost struck me dead. Name not ye word Money, and you'l see I shall soone grow well.

---

[134] Catchwords, "I am," for fols. 42–42v.
[135] Obsolete variant of "quickly."

CRA: You shall haue y^{r} will. Sit here a[nd] take y^{r} rest till I returne. Ile get you something to strengthen y^{r} sicke stomack.

exit

STR: Now I'm well enough. All my sicknes is vanisht. The ffort is taken, and I haue got ye Prize. Deceit must be answered with deceit. Now tis best for me to be gon; for I know ye conditions of my Mother; as soone as she perceives how egregiously she is cousen'd, she['ll] breake into a rage. I am now well, she presently will haue her turne of sicknesse.

exit

Sce: 9.

Crabula.

enter Cra: with a Caudell[136]

My Strumbo, drinke vs this whilst tis hot. But here's nobody. Strumbo where art? Whither is he now gon? Has he hid himselfe? Has he deceu'd me? Is he run away? And did he delude me with flattering words? Doe all things apeare to me in a Mist? I am much afraid he has vs'd some cunning deceit. Alas! So it is. I am vtterly vndon! My Money! My purse! All, he hath stolen away. Woe is me! This was the reason of his sickness, to turn it vpon me. O wicked Rogue! Bloodsucking Rascall! Theeuing villain! What[137] shall I doe now? Goe hang my selfe for a simple, [fol. 43]
foolish woman. But Ile after him; and bring him to a due Correction.

exit

Sce: 10.

S$^{t.}$ Cuthbert. Alfrede.

S$^{t.}$ Cuth: apears to Alf: in his sleepe

Heau'ns triumphant Rector, infusing strength
into y^{e} breasts of Kings; whose awfull hand

---

[136] That is, "caudle"—a warm drink, especially for an ill person.
[137] Catchword, uncapitalized in MS, for fols. 42v–43.

guides the raines of the Vniverse, hath sent
me from heau'n to bring you ye gratefull message
of Peace: I am that Cuthbert, whose aide you
so oft implor'd in y^{r} extremities;
and whom with one loafe wch was all that you
had left, charitably you fed. By these
Deedes you haue mitigated Gods Anger
who mindfull of ye restitution
of his beloued England, fertille with
so numerous a progeny of Saints,
hath prepared new triumphs, and new Kingdoms.
Let this be an assured marke of y^{r} future
Conquest[—] that y^{r} Landlord shall returne
loaded with a great quantity of fish,
And y^{r} soldiers impale[138] you with their troopes;
then goe to wars. And put y^{r} Confidence
in th' Omnipotent hand wch fights for you.

S$^{t.}$ Cuth: disapears

ALF: O venerated Patrone! O Cuthbert,
the Glory of my Cuntry! The fortresse
and pillar of my life, whither fly you?
Before you penetrate y^{e} Clouds, O take
my pious intents; and offer vp to God
this Gift: if my Cuntry may be free'd
from its miseries, and I once againe [fol. 43v]
enioy my Kingdome, in this verry Place
Ile Consecrate a Temple to your Name,
One, rich in Marble, the discourse of all
Ages, and admir'd by y^{e} whole world.
My life is not now so vnfortunate,
Since Gods potent hand prepares redresses;
Heau'n fights for me; and all things generously
conspire to afford [r]e[l]iefe to my griefs.

Sce: 11.

Osberga. Alfrede.

I had a dreame represented strange things
to my imagination. S$^{t.}$ Cuthbert
appearing told me with a reall voice

[138] Meaning, not to pierce, but to enclose or surround.

you should be reinstaul'd in Englands Throne.
O my thrice happy Age; if yet at length
after these sad afflictions of life
it hath deserv'd to see y^{t} welcome Day!
ALF: The same Aparition of S$^{t.}$ Cuthbert
presented itselfe in my sleepe, and gaue
me evident signes of future triumphs.
But Denevulph's return'd, and Comes as if
he brought some newes.

Sce: 12.

Denevulphe. Alfrede.
Osberga.

My Guest, I am Come to tell you strang Newes,
and a wonder; going out with my Netts
in a season much vnfavorable
for fishing, and casting them in a Pond,
on a suddain, there fell into ye Netts
A vast qua[n]tity of fish wch almost [fol. 44]
broke the Nets and for'ct them back into ye water;
with no small labour we puld ashore;
New cause of wonder did then arise,
when we saw ye Number was so great, it
might sufficiently haue fed a Multitude.
ALF: Tis ye Event of my Dreame wch you relate,
and the signe of my future victories.

Sce: 13.

Edward. Humfrey. Athelrede.
Alfrede. Souldiers. Denevulphe.

Whilst neere ye Rising of the sun I vew'd
ye wood, an army of Souldiers did
Appeare; Humfrey Generall of ye horse
and Athelrede of the foote, lead on these
Martiall troopes collected for y^{r} service.
HUM: As you commanded me (when, hauing lost
ye battell, to avoide the Enimy
you were necessitated to betake
y^{r} selfe to flight vnattended) I strait
Collected fforces through ye whole Kingdome

which brauely haue resolv'd in y^{r} service
either to dye, or regaine their Cuntry,
and restore you to your pristine Glory.
ALF: I do acknowledge ye truth of my vision.
ATHEL: I here returne ye sacred Diadem
wch you com̃itted to my charge: and haue
prepar'd regall and splendid Robes, for you.
The Souldiers expresse their loyalty
to their New found King, and congratulate [fol. 44v]
y^{r} welcome with their Acclamations.
SOUL: God saue King Alfrede.
DEN: My Liege. I most humbly kneele for Pardon
that ignorantly I treated you at
my house not as it became y^{r} regall
dignity.
ALF: Rise Denevulphe; I esteeme thee as a friend[;]
the memory of thy charity to me
shall ever liue within my gratefull breast:
and be an example to externs;[139] and
a document to ye posterity
of future Ages, not that thou hast
entertaind with hospitality
a triumphant King; but hast faithfully
with food and lodging releev'd one Needy
Miserable, and exil'd. Wherefore thou
shalt follow vs. I promise to maintaine
thy family at my Cost, who fed'st mine
at thy expences. Now, Stout Mars's Crew,
vnder heaun's Conduct lets ye wars renew.[140]

exeunt

Sce: 14.

Edelvitha. Elgina.

Who taught that Loue produces iealous feares
was no false prophete; nor absented from
ye limits of verity. This, a loue
to a Husband, so immense as mine

[139] "Situated in or belonging to foreign countries" or by extension. "Not belonging to a specified community; that is a non-member"—*OED*, s.v. "extern."

[140] Scenes in *Alfrede* are not usually concluded with a rhyme as this one is. The metaphor of "Stout Mars's Crew" is Knightley's.

Confirms by a severe experience.
FFeare permits not my anxious thoughts
to fix on any resolue. It represents
fflights, banishments, ye horrid Menaces
of blacke Night, my Son lost, with his Sister, [fol. 45]
and my Husband retreated into the
watry Marshes o'th' Isle Athelnea.
Alas! What part of all my breast remaines
vnassaulted[,] wch feare and loue distracts,
and raging griefe peirces, and a beliefe
too credulous of threat'ning Misfortunes[?]
But now my Hart's grown stout, obdurated
by so many sorrows; now stopping the
sluces[141] of my teares, couragiously
I dare, accompanied with Elgine[,]
walke though ye open fields, and travell ye
darke Recesses of solitary woods;
and take a iourney towards Athelnea[,]
Leauing ye protection of a Castle
whose security is now vnsecure
that I may enioy ye sight of Alfrede,
and receiue his vltimate embraces.
ELG: This Place, Mother, invites vs to refresh
our wearied limbes with a little rest[;]
This is ye Cell of the venerable
Neothus, wch yeelds hospitality
to Pilgrims. Let's goe into it, before
ye skeys are overspread with darker Clouds
and ye hollow winds produce tempestuous
showers. I heare, the Concaues of the wood
Commence a dreadfull Murmur. And ye earth
allready shakes with loud groans of thunder[;]
lets goe in, till a serener day,
vnclouds ye sun, and expells the tempest.
EDE: Although my mind be disturbed with no [fol. 45v]
small feares presaging the Omen of some
approaching misfortune coutch'd within these
menaces of the Skyes and blustring winds;
yet this oportunity, and the great
sanctity of this Hermite invite me

---

[141] Variant of "sluices," which is "A channel, drain, or small stream, *esp.* one carrying off overflow or surplus water"—*OED*, s.v. "sluice."

to goe in. The Dore is open, nor is
there an appearance of any body.
ELG: Perhaps he's gon elsewhere to say his prayres.
EDE: Wee therefore will here expect his returne
they goe in
till ye storme be past, and ye day clearer.

Sce: 15.

Rollo.

FFortune, thou'st too bountifully enricht
thy Client: what an India of treasures
Doth here present itselfe? How much will this
Ingratiate me with Gothurnus? Who will
Confer not onely a Pardon, but wealth
and honours on me, by whose hand Alfred's queene
togeather with the princesse his Daughter
enter soul[d]iers
shall become Captiues to his ambition.
Behold; the rage of ye tempest hath brought
my Companions to ye refuge of
this sheltring wood; Come hither, my friends[;]
fortune at length hath crown'd our hopes; we hold
ye Prey wch must ransome our liberties,
and yeeld vs life, and glory. Whilst by chance
vpon the top of a high hill, I vew'd
ye vallies, and fields, and adiacent woods,
I saw two women running in great hast [fol. 46]
through those Meadows where ye river
silently hastens to encorporate
it selfe with the Noble streames of [Athelnea.]
I vigilantly followed them, shrowding
myselfe behind ye interposed trees
least any eye should haue discovered
my stealth: when they came to this place, I knew
by their discourse, that it was Alfreds queene
and his daughter, wch were arrived here;
Now, to avoide ye storme, they are entred
that little Cell, wch presently will yeeld
an Entry to our triumphs. Why do. I
thus protract delayes in speaking? My ffriends
you that haue followed me, y^{r} Captaine

in hardship, behold what treasures attend
y^{r} liberty. But none of vs must use
the least violence: they must our freedome bring
and are design'd as presents for the King.

exeunt

Sce: 16.

Osberne. Gormo.

What do's this suddain change of weather
portend? [—]the sun invelopt in black clouds,
the windes raging, th' earth made into a sea,
by the unsluc'd[142] flood gates of ye weeping heauns.
When I ruminate on these things, I am
at a stand and know not their certaine Cause.
Sense is stupify'd and reason must yeeld
Inferiour to the eternall Councells.
Such distempers in ye skeys arise not [fol. 46v]
but design'd for some intent; either for
a Caution to deterre vs from our Crimes;
or by Cristalline showers to fertillize
the growing fields.—
GOR: I'm not at all sollicitous why God
terrifyes ye world with such Menaces[;]
My Care is onely to amend my life
wch makes me dubious what to avoide,
and what to follow being a Tyro
newly enlisted vnder Christs banners;
for an innate storme more tempestuously
rages within me purging ye fetidies[143]
of vice from out ye Center of my breast
then that wch swells the sea, and shakes ye earth,
breaking from ye spungy wombe of ye Clouds.
OSB: Neothus hath apply'd a remedy
to those wounds, lucidly demonstrating
the path to life: he adviced vs to assume
this pilgrims habit, a proper garment
for penitents. He[,] foreseeing the greatnesse

---

[142] See 4.14.18n.

[143] "The quality or state of being fetid; a fetid nature or condition; foulness, ill savour, offensiveness"—*OED*, s.v. "fetidity."

of this storme[,] bid vs goe home before him[.]
GOR: But heare. A Noise comes from ye Cell[;] what do they
within? I heare ye outcries and Complaints of women[.]
OSB: Let vs remaine a while in this place.
I see some Danish souldiers coming forth;
ye first is Rollo leading two women manicle'd.
GOR: What a sun of beauty shines
through ye clouds of that homely decency!
Tis no ignoble Prize. Wee'l see ye event.

Sce: 17 [fol. 47]

Rollo. Soldiers. Edelvitha.
Elgine.

Come forward (Queene) why make you these demurs?
Y^r iourney is from one King to another.
Alfrede liues exil'd from his owne Kingdome.
Hee's depos'd, trample'd on, miserable,
One not worth envy, a vagabond;
ffortune hath provided better for you[,]
wch out of this despeare will raise you to
Gothurnus, a Man worthy of Englands Crowne.
He victoriously sits in that throne
from which Alfrede is fallen: thus ffortune
Giues and takes by turnes: One scepter admits
not two hands. Why doe teares swell y^r eyes?
Why grioue you? Y^r misery is now past.
'Twill be a happinesse to become a
Prisoner to a victorious King:
you'l finde an easy condescention
to your supplications; a pious
Mercy to y^r afflictions; in fine
a Noble generosity both to
y^r selfe and y^r daughter. Perhaps he may
become Alfred's son-in-law[;] restore him
to his Kingdome, and seat him in his throne.
EDE: O severe Censurer! O too austere
too cruell an arbitrator of our
Misfortunes! Vnder what Clymat; or in
what wildernesse were you nurst? Certainly
by some salvage Animall. Can you then [fol. 47v]
imagine this in affliction to be

A Comfort? [—]for a Queene thus to become
A Captiue to an impious Tyrant?
And a virgin to be presented
to an adulterer? What inhuman
or barbarous Inhabitant of the
most remote and vnciviliz'd Cuntry
would not even blush at ye wickednesse
of this Resolve? O change, vnlesse y^{r} hart
be made of stone, or y^{r} breast of Iron,
O Change your cruel Resolution:
If you want arguments to induce y^{r} minde
to a resentment, Imagine her to be
y^{r} owne Mother, wch thus bound you force
along; and this your sister, strait to be
violated by a Ravisher.
Can you suffer so great an infamy?
I know you would abhorre it; nor would you
permit y^{r} owne blood to be stained with
such dishonour; but much rather defend
their ffame with a vindicatiue hand.
If it be a slight Motiue that I am
a Queene, suppose mee to be y^{r} Mother[;]
if this be too much, imagine, I am
y^{r} Client; and if not that, y^{r} servant:
but if this you iudge to high a title
deeme me ye most despised of y^{r} slaues,
what'ere deserves ye Name of beggarly,
Poor, base, low, vile, and abiect that Ile bee;
Nay Ile be nothing. Giue me any Name
Or none at all, so that I may avoide [fol. 48]
the adulterous hands of Gothurnus,
and may not see my daughters Chastity
Contaminated by his impurities.
Why deny you my iust supplications?
I beg not to avoid death but Infamy.
She that desires death feares not to dy.
Tis a glory to dye for Honours sake.
I aske, you'l either free me of my life
Or of this Infamy; I care not which[.]
You may doe both[;] in doing either you'l
make me happy[;] if you condescend to both,
Riches and honours shall attend on you,
scepters and Kings shall be at y^{r} Command.
Will not this perswade? If words are of no force

let my teares become better Orators;
Let vertue, let piety plead for me.
ROLL: Piety? Tis but an empty Name you
obiect. I would know where tis to be found:
vnlesse a wickednesse be Pious, I
acknowledge Piety to be nowhere.
Nor doe I esteeme any thing pious
abstracted from vtility; he that
regards vertue and Piety follows
airy shadows, and empty nullities.
What doe you tell me of these sterile Goods[?]
Y^{r} ffame? Y^{r} honour? Meere trifles, nothing.
Vertue is to be contemn'd where neither
Pleasure, nor profit is conioyn'd with it.
EDE: Pleasure and profit are to be contemn'd
where vertue is not their Companion.
ROLL: O vitious vertue! Full of tyranny, [fol. 48v]
Amaritude,[144] toyle, and difficulty!
Why should that checke vs from doing w^{t} we please?
Ile doe what ere my sense doth suggest.
EDE: Reason ought to bridle Sense.
ROL: Reason's but weake where ye will makes Resolues.
EDE: Tis ye property of irrationall
Animalls to be guided by Sense.
Reason should direct a prudent Man.
ROL: Reason directs me to follow my profit.
EDE: But that Reason's blinde.
ROL: It promises me Pardon, and honours
too, if I present you to Gothurnus.
EDE: Alfrede will give you all this.
ROL: Yes. A bannisht Man!
EDE: Yet liues, to be reveng'd.
ROL: Hee's inferiour in War.
EDE: But superiour in Courage.
ROL: His Courage is to little purpose.
EDE: Tis yet to be feared.
ROL: A fugitiue to be feared?
EDE: Because he liues.
ROL: Let him liue, contemn'd by his enimies:
Let him still want his wife, Children, and Kingdome,
and let him see his daughter and his queene

---

[144] Obsolete for "bitterness."

given vp to be adulterated:[145]
whatever wickednesse one enimy
doth to another, tis a pious deede.
Wherefore follow, or Il drag you after me.
Enter. Osb: Gor: each snatches a
sword and makes ye sol: run away
OSB: Wherefore dye.
Disburthen ye earth of so much wickednes.
Hath ye villain 'scap't his deserved death? [fol. 49]
GOR: His Comrades are also run after their Leader.
OSB: But heau'ns iust vengence will overtake them.
Disconsolate Queene, collect y^r senses,
for those you fear'd, feare hath vanquisht.
EDE: Generous Hero's, I know not how,
or in what gratefull manner to addresse
myselfe to you. As a tender Mother,
beholding her deare Childe in safety (which
floating vpon ye tempestuous seas
in a totter'd vessel she imagin'd
to be absorp't by ye devouring waues,
or at least cast vpon some vnknown Clymat)
Can scarse divest herselfe of feare, although
she see's him; and still fancies his abscence
whose presence she enioyes[;] so I, whom griefe
had almost made dispeare, am yet doubtfull
whether really I see this wellcome succour,
Or ye Image of some dreame deludes my sight:
my Minde's not yet vnclog'd with feare, and yet
I see no enimy, no Cause to feare.
But you, from whom no imaginary
assistance hath accrew'd to our succour,
what adorations shall we make you?
What retributions shall wee returne?
Shall we belieue you'r Angells come from heau'n,
or shall we Call you Mortalls?
OSB: These penitent Weedes declare vs Mortall,
and that we haue bin guilty of misdeedes:
but ye holly documents of Neothus
haue reclaim'd vs from ye paths of errour
and consequently from Death: and hath made [fol. 49v]

---

[145] Meaning, "raped," "ravished." On the relation of this term to the concepts of "degeneration" and "mutability" see "Critical Interpretation."

vs participant of ye divine light
of faith. He foreknowing y^{r} distresses,
far from hence bid vs goe home. But, he's come
with more then ordinary pleasantnesse.
EDE: Lets goe to him—

Sce: 1[8].

Edelvitha. Neothus. Osberne.
Gormo. Elgine.

O holy Neothus. Thou Refuge of
safety, to th' desolate Britans; Behold
a Queene, wretched, miserable, a prey
to Enimies, depriv'd of her husband,
destitute of her Children, and vnlesse
you had free'd vs from this last extremity
with reliefe, a designed Prostitute
to th' pleasure of an Enimy. Alas!
When will our afflictions and miseries
haue an end? Instruct me what I shall doe,
Or what I may hope for.
NEO: Wonder not, if the vnhappy State
of life be pervious to afflictions.
For heau'n hath given this law to Mortalls
that no sublunary thing shall be fixt,
or permanent. We see ye Clouds disgorge
themselves of raine; ye earth by ye impulse
of waues dislocated; the aspiring sea
sweld into ye skyes; and ye ponderous earth
scarce (thô so im̃ense a bulke) endures
ye batteries of ye violent windes. [fol. 50]
Y^{e} Nature even of things Insensitiue
suffers variation; nor ye Elements
of ye celestiall Orbes are exempted
from viciscitude: why therefore in the
revolution of human life should
we wonder if prosperity be mixt
with adversity; good with ill; th' highest
with ye lowest; and ioy and sorrow doe
alternately prevaile. Life can promise
nothing secure; He's free alone from feare
and triumphs ore ye world that liues vnmou'd

and vnconcern'd at ye change of fortune;
who knows how to bridle his desires,
and regulate ye passions of his Minde;
who leauing earthly for eternall Goods,
hoards vp an vncreased Treasure.
Now heare what af[t]er y^r Calamities
you must hope for. I bring you ioyfull Newes[—]
Know that y^r husband, Children, Mother,
and all y^r princely stocke are in Safety:
and know that there is a potent Army
of souldiers not far from this place, vnder
their ensignes, all ready to execute
ye Commands of Alfrede. Fortune is revers't,
Triumphs decreed by heau'n attend Alfrede.
A most iust revenge of ye divine hand
hath also overtooke those barbarians
wch even now escap't by flight, when they [fol. 50v]
intended to present you and Elgine
to Gothurnus: but some brittish souldiers
meeting, and stoutly encountring them,
haue taken them prisoners and now in
a dungeon, such as they intended for you
they expiate that wickednesse in chaines.
EDEL: O blest fortune! What thankes shall I returne
to God and you? My breast is too narrow
to lodge so much ioy. I stand astonisht
at this strange newes: wch raises me aboue myselfe.
NEO: O Queene command y^r selfe; when good ffortune
abounds reflect on ill: and moderate
y^r ioy[;] let that and sorrow haue a like
Reception in y^r hart, least the one
too much deiects y^r minde, and ye other
doth vanity and insolency bring.
But now tis time to goe and meet ye King.

exeunt.

Act: 5.

Sce: i.

Alfrede. Humfrey.
Souldiers.

all like misitians

We goe as yet vnobserv'd by any,
And march through ye midst of our enimies
vnmolested: The Victour lyes buried
in sleepe vpon the grasse. Nobody stands
Sentinell. The Captaines are all intent
vpon their frolickes, and recreations;
The Souldiers vnarm'd giue themselves to rest,
some feasting, some drinking, others at Play:
In fine ev'ry one thinkes himselfe secure.
HUM: Idlenesse is oft bought at a deare rate. [fol. 51]
And ease is an ill gaurd[146] to victory.
As a credulous Mariner, when the
Sky is serene, commits his ship to th' winds
which swell ye pregnant sailes with a stife[147] gale:
Strait, if their too rough blasts shake his vessell,
and accumulate mountaines in ye seas,
an unexpected terrour ceases him,
and he then curses ye deluding windes.
Even so ye warlike sound of trumpets
calls ye danes from their negligent rest to armes:
they'l learne at their owne cost how treacherous
is their too much presum'd security
and with how great inconstancy, fortune
disposeth of y^e lots of victory,
seldome admitting a lasting happinesse.
ALF: See, we are come neere Gothurnus his tent.
His Pages are coming forth.

---

[146] Variant of "guard."
[147] Obsolete form of "stiff."

Sce: 2.

Pipero. Titmus. Alfrede.
Humfrey. etc.

Titmus, seest thou how all things goe totsy=[/]turvy[148] since griefe or rather madnesse possest our King proceeding from y^{e} death of his brother and Kinsman? He cares not for his Armes as he was wont, nor delights he in his horses[,] nor fortify's his Tents, nor sends out Scouts, nor encourages his souldiers, but some times he's as mute as a fish, and sometimes exclaimes as loud as thunder. He groanes, sighs, grieues, threatens, and rages[.]

ALF: How impatiently an insolent Tyrant endures adversity; [fol. 51v]

PIP: Yet ye coming of ye souldier wch affirm'd that he had kil'd King Alfrede was something oportune.

ALF: What's this? Is't rumor'd that I'm also Kild?

PIP: Twas Alfrede's Robes wch made him be belieu'd.

ALF: What Robes? Perhaps those wch in my flight I threw into a Pit.

PIP: He had a thousand[149] pounds for his rewar'd.

ALF: T'was a prosperous lye.

PIP: And now he's made one of y^{e} Kings Guard.

TIT: Now Pipero, you touch vpon a businesse hatefull to me. As though that word=thundring Gyant, could overcome King Alfrede, much lesse kill him; who dares not cry Hisse to a goose. His hands are more apt for theevery then war: wherefore, I conclude, that he stole those Robes, and got them not by force.— Doe you remember with what opprobrious language he affronted me, becaus I was not attentiue to his Commands? How he cald me the excrement of a Mouse, and lesse then nothing[,] nay brag'd, he would eat me vp with veneger like pickeld herring[?] Ile no longer endure these Affronts: but am Resolv'd to dare him to y^{e} fyld.[150] Wherefore Ile send him this chalenge writ in this Paper. And you shall carry it.— Ile make him know that I doe not degenerate from y^{e} noble Progeny of Pigmies.

[PIP]: Ile carry it. But first let me read it. Titmus to Polemobombardifragosogiganio=[/]machopumponides

[148] That is, "topsy-turvy."

[149] The extraordinary sum, in pounds, is obviously anachronistic.

[150] Variant for "field."

sends Revenge. Althô this title hath taken vp a whole side, lets goe on to y^{e} rest. Hadst thou as many feete as thy [fol. 52] Name is compos'd of, they would all be few enough to carry thee from my indignation. Know that I am thy mor=[/]tall enimy. Nor doth thy monstrous Name hinder me from Chalenging thee to a duell. If thou wauest fighting where I finde thee Ile put a Halter about thy necke and drag thee along y^{e} streets; and shew thee to y^{e} poeple for a strange Monster: If thou accept it, Ile bridle thee like an Asse, and will get vpon thy backe and ride thee. FFarewell, till I make you fare ill.
Titmus thy words bite worse then a Louse.

TIT: But my deedes shall bite worse then my words.

PIP: Hee himselfe is now coming this way.

Sce: 3. #:

Bragadocia. Pipero. Titmus.
Alfrede. Humfrey. etc.

Give roome here to ye invincible Champion of Gothurnus, coming to expatiate abroad. What doe these gnats doe here? Get yee out of my sight ye pitifull wormes.

PIP: Reade this, Monstrous Giant.

delivers ye Chalenge

BRA: Whats this? What mortall is so foolish to contend wth me?

TIT: Tis I, great Collossus, who thus contem[n]e thee and thy Pride.

BRA: Oh. Oh. they'l teare me to peeces.

ALFE: They'l teare my cloaths to peeces.
Humfrey[,] lets not suffer this man to be tormented to death by thes two wasps. Stop now y^{r} rage[;] he hath sufficiently felty^{r} anger.

TIT: Let me alone[;] I haue not yet satisfyed my revenge. [fol. 52v]

PIP: My wrath boiles within me[;] let me power it forth vpon this immense Bulke.

BRA: Joue, vnframe ye vniverse, brandish thy Lightning: exenterate[151] the Articke,

[151] "To take out the entrails of; to eviscerate, disembowel"—*OED*, s.v. "exenterate."

and antarticke Poles of Haile as big as
Milstones and eiaculate[152] them vpon
Atla[s]'s shoulders, that brus'd with ponderous
Contusions, he may sinke vnder ye heaun's,
and confound all things, that the world may be
revers'd into its primitiue Chaos:
for I am all in a raging ffury.

PIP: Wee'l give him leaue to talke. Let vs goe in.

ex. Pip: Tit:

Sce: 4.

Pimpo. Bragadocia. Alfrede.
Humfrey.

enter, Pim.

Whats the reason that my Master lookes about with such truculent eyes?

BRA: Now I could tosse those Mountaines Pindus and Ossa[153] like tennis Balls:

PIM: Master what thus exasperates you?

BRA: And throw 'em at Jupiters Head.

PIM: Are you in y^r senses?

BRA: Ile let loose the Giants from their Prisons.

PIM: You are furious[.]

[ALF]: Ile coniure downe his ffury with one word. Harke hither—Alfrede liues. Be gon.

BRA: Woe's is me! Pimpo lets hast away[.]

exit

PIM: How suddainly hee is vanish't. My Master threatens and runs away all in a breath.

exit

HUM: His anger is turned into feare, and he is grown patient of a suddain.

ALF: He thought it his best course to be gon, least when [fol. 53] Gothurnus vnderstands his deceit, he may sustain ye punishment of it. However by his fallacy he hath cous'ned

---

[152] In this context, "To dart or shoot forth; to throw out suddenly and swiftly, eject"—*OED*, s.v. "ejaculate."

[153] Mountains in Thessaly. To pile Pindus on Ossa is to put mountain on top of mountain. Bragadocia emphasizes the ease with which he can accomplish these titanic feats.

our enimy of a thousand pound. The Kings at hand. His Pages come with him. Tis time you within tune y^r instruments, and prepare ye dance. Ile observe his strange lookes, speeches, and gestures, and will diligently search into the secrets of his bosome. How horridly he rowles[154] his distracted eyes.

Sce: 5.

Gothurnus, Osberne. Gormo.
Alfrede.

osb: Gor: disguis'd

Shall I complain[,] or with the loud Clamour
of an angry voice fill ye aire, ye fields,
and ecchoing vallies? I could deplore
the losse of Osberne, but my rage forbids:
griefe and anger cruelly teare my brest
with contrary impulses. A doubtfull suspense
impedes my resolues: grife tells me, 'tis best
to condole his sad funerall with teares,
and complaine oth' Cruelty of ye Gods:
Anger cry's out, Stand at a defyance,
and execrate their perfidiousnesse:
Griefe perswades me to lament my brother[;]
Anger reproves me, and askes if teares can
bring a remedy: timerous women
can doe as much— Grow desperate, and arme
thy hand with some audacious attempt.
Even as two Combating windes divide
ye sea with oposite Agitations, [fol. 53v]
and sometimes the one forces ye reeling waues,
sometimes, ye other confus'dly driues them
in concatenated mountains to ye Shore;
yet dubious whose Summons to obey:
So 'twixt ye flames of anger, and ye streames
of teares my wau'ring mind floates vnresolv'd.
What shall I determine, Rage, or Lament?
Ile Rage, and lament too. My breast shall feele
th' impetuositie of Both their assaults;
Ile be enflam'd with rage, and drown'd in teares.

[154] Obsolete variant of "rolls."

that a grieuing Rage, and a raging griefe,
may totally possesse my bosome.
OSB: Suppresse y^{r} impotent ffury. That which
yôu lament, you lament in vaine; for that
wch you rage y^{r} Rage vanisheth into ye aire.
What death hath once devour'd cant be regain'd;
tis then against y^{r} selfe alone that you
excite y^{r} anger.
GOTH: Griefe communicated somewhat abates
the intemp'rate motions of ye minde.
OSB: But rage incensed renews it againe.
GOTH: Doe you then dissuade me from lamenting
so deere a Brother?
OSB: I disswade you
from grieuing with too violent a griefe.
GOTH: True loue admits no limits in griefe.
OSB: True loue admits not any griefe at all.
GOTH: What most we loue we most lament.
OSB: Where we loue ill.
GOTH: He that laments his friend loues well.
OSB: We grieue for ill things not for good.
GOTH: We grieue for good things that are lost.
OSB: If lost will griefe recouer them?
GOTH: Who are you, that would thus limit my griefe? [fol. 54]
OSB: I am a Dane, and now follow y^{r} Conduct.
I was (I must confesse) A Companion
to Haldain, Hubba, and Hingar, three Kings,
which being lately kild by ye brittans,
hard fortune hath brought me hither
accompanied with one friend.
GOTH: I entertaine you both as my deare friends
because you are in misery, and are come
to one more miserable then y^{r} selues.
I resent y^{r} misfortune, and alone
will grieue for myselfe; my sorrows need not
your condolement. The perpetuall losse
of Osbern is mine.

ye mu: play and others begin to dance

ALF: Now play y^{r} parts.—
Lead vp the dance, and foote it with
an actiue nimblenesse.—Light tunes please not,
begin other Dances to sollemn aires.
GOTH: Enough. Be gon.
ALF: Lets goe. His Countenance lookes grim, as if
enflam'd with an angry passion.

Our trumpets will presently sound a tune
to another Dance, wch he dreames not of.
GOTH: Shall I allwayes sloathfully thus remaine
plung'd in the same perplexities? And shall
I endure it? Shall ye iust fury
of Gothurnus disquiet nobody
but himselfe? Shall I still complain, and dye
without revenge? My dearest Brother fell
by ye bloody hand of an Enimy;
and shall I not persue that Enimy
with fire and sword? Shall not my souldiers
hast[e] to their Armes; and consume to ashes
townes, Cities, Houses, yea and temples too?
Noe small Riuer of Blood can quench so great [fol. 54v]
a Thirst[;] vast seas shall flow: in Britanie
itselfe, one Britane shall'nt be found aliue:
England shall be its owne funerall flame,
and lye buried in its owne ashes:
Alfrede shall become food for ravenous
vultures to prey vpon. Edward his son
shall feele my Revenge. Shall then feele it,
and doth not? Doe's he feele it, and hath not
already felst it? O my Sluggish Soule!
Ere this, ye enimy should haue paid their liues
to my revenge; now tis almost too late[;]
however it shall overtake them. And I
surrounded with a sea of blood will laugh
and make a consort with their howling groanes.

Sce: 6.

Messenger. Gothurnus. Osberne.
Gormo.

Alfrede liues—
GOTH: Villain thou stabst me. Canst thou tell me that?
MES: And what's more, hee's well.
GOTH: Is there anything more yet?
MES: There is[.]
GOTH: What ist?
MES: At this instant he leades his numerous troopes
into your Tents, and preys vpon ye spoile[,]

who even now disguis'd in ye habit
of a Musitian prepar'd dances in y^r presence.
GOTH: O Gods! Where's he, who affirm'd that
with his owne hand he had Kild that King
and brought away his Robes?
MES: He's run away.
GOTH: Am I then deluded[,] and cheated with
ye specious fallacy of a lye? [fol. 55]
I, a Conquerour; thus su[b]du'd by deceit[,]
periury, by my owne souldiers, and by
the armes of an Enimy. How low
am I basely suncke? Abiect Gothurnus!
What dost thou doe, seest thou, and know'st thou this?
I am not; nor doe I draw vitall breath.
I am now amongst ye infernall vmbra's:
Here Cocytus, and there Styx vomit vp
their soutty waues: and, that extinguisher
of Cares, Lethe[155] environs me with a
soporiferous Cloude. Y^e are all Ghosts;
Charon,[156] Hells waterman will Strait be here,
to wit ye Enimy, are waft vs ore
ye infernall Lakes.
SOUL: Arme. Arme. The Enimies at hand.
within[157]
GOTH[:] What confused noyse sounds in my eares
And harshly calls to Armes? Whats this? I see
ye flight of souldiers of my owne.
O horrid shame! Stand. Or this hand shall giue
that death from wch you run. FFearfull Cowards!
Doe you feare y^r enimies? I am one.
He dyes that comes another step this way.
Timerous soules! Hartlesse Danes! Vnmindfull
of glory! Are ye affraid of those, who
lye almost at ye mercy of y^r swords?
Will Conquerours run from ye Conquered?
O face about. Y^r flight's degenerous.
And ye safety you seeke more dangerous:
Where there is no refuge; where naked swords
gaurd ev'ry angle. If yee will choose death,

---

155 River of forgetfulness in Hades.

156 Ferryman of the underworld.

157 A clear indication that the concretely-imagined staging calls for an inner as well as an outer area.

my hand shall give it, if life y^r owne.
Let life be y^r election, death is
a due to our Enimies. Liue equall [fol. 55v]
to y^r triumphs. Y^r conquering swords haue gain'd
A lawrell[;] let y^r Courage mantain[158] it.
Victors must defend their spoiles. Learn of me,
y^r Leader, either to dye gloriously,
or to win honour from an enimy,
halfe conquered already. Y^e shall purchase
victory or death by my example.

SOUL: We all follow.

exeunt all but pip: Tit:

Sce: 7.

Titmus. Pipero.

Now pipero, whilst they are in the heat of battel let vs do an exploit worthy of our Names.

PIP: What ist Titmus?

TIT: Lets pursue Bragadocia with all our might and bring him backe to ye King bound like A Calfe.

PIP: Lets goe then. Fame shall trumpet forth this attempt. I swell with animosity against him.

exeunt

Sce: 8.

Gothurnus. Alfrede. Osberne
Gormo. Humfrey. Athelrede.
Souldiers.

Alfrede, defend y^r selfe.

ALF: That Counsell best befits Gothurnus.

GOTH: I'm come to call thee to a resignement of thy Crowne long since due, of thy life, and of Osberne.

they fight
Goth: with his [crown?] retreates into a Castle

---

[158] Obsolete variant of "maintain."

ALF: Win it and were[159] it—
The Enimy is fled into ye Castle.
Y^{e} preys entrapt: we must prepare a siege.

exeunt

Sce: 9 # [fol. 56]

Pimpo.

with a bag of money

That wch is due to the profit of servants when their masters are too covetous, or so prodigall that they leaue nothing to giue to vs, I haue now fullfild it; hauing stolen away my Masters money: but least he should dye intestate, I haue left him some, that if he should want a halter to hang himselfe, he may presently furnish himselfe with one: Now I am a free man: Money makes men free. You may iudge whither[160] I more serv'd my Master or my selfe. By my ingenuity he cosened Gothurnus of this money[;] now by my wisdome it falls out that y^{e} profit redounds to me. Now if my Master be well, it is well, I am well; and bid you all farewell. For somebody is coming this way.

exit

Sce: 10.

Strumbo.

Now am I a man three stories high. A Rusticke, A Souldier, and A Courtier; but as yet my capacity is got no higher then the first: how=[/]ever this sword proclames me a souldier, but I neither know how to fight, nor doe I desire to be instructed, vnlesse men would take more care of hurting one another. To speake y^{e} truth I haue bin trying this halfe hower to draw my sword out of y^{e} scabbard, wch has put me into this sweat; but I belieue a yolk of oxen can scarse get it out; and so much y^{e} better. 'Twill[161] be a good [fol. 56v]

---

[159] Obsolete variant of wear.
[160] Meaning "whether."
[161] Catchword, uncapitalized in MS, for fols. 56–56v.

excuse to avoid fighting; for if any=[/]body should fall vpon me before I can draw my sword I may then honorably cry quarter. These gay Cloaths speake me a Courtier, but I haue not yet perfectly learnt to ly, like a courtier, to flatter, to dissemble, to complement and court ladies, to sleepe after dinner, to sweare, and sometimes be forsworen, to game, to cheate, to be in loue, to adore a Mistresse, to kisse her hand, to cringe and congie,[162] to smell of perfumes, and a thou=[/]sand other apish tricks wch I ca'nt remember. I am now going along with my Mother to wait vpon the Kings Mother, and ye young Princesse. But I had rather be amongst my hogs again, or tumbling our Joane,[163] then vse such ridicu=[/]lous postures, and fasshions, as these great gen=[/]tle folkes expect: and yet my Mother is so in loue with these phantasticall divises,[164] that I feare, ere long she'l grow mad[;] Im sure she is not herselfe allready for she lookes forty yeares younger then she did two days agoe[;] her tawny complexion is chang'd into pure red and white, wch she takes at plea=[/]sure out of a Box. She hath also got a set of new teeth, wch she layes aside at night and sets them in ranke and file again next mor=[/]ning. To day she spent no lesse then fiue houres in dressing of herselfe before a lookinglasse; where, 'twas ye brauest sport to see into what strange fashions she windes, and turnes her coun=[/]tenance; now she dislikes ye setteing of her mouth, now this haire is out of order now t'other Beauty spot must be set in a more gracefull place; Is not this rare[,] to see one that was wont to[165] weare patches vpon her peticote, now [fol. 57]
weare them vpon her face[?] But here she comes.

enter Cra:

If yee desire to see a Compendium of ye whole Court, looke vpon her well.

---

[162] Sometimes rendered congee—ceremonious leave-taking or dismissal.

[163] Meaning, "have intercourse with [Joane]." Joan is a frankly sexual name used to signify a loose (country) woman.

[164] That is, "devices."

[165] Catchword for fols. 56v–57.

Sce: 11.

Crabula. Strumbo.

Strumbo hold my ffan—now restore it to me, and take my hood.

STR: Hold, Restore, Take[—] these certainly are Court words.

CRA: Ah! I am now a little weary[;] hold thy Mother by the Arme—now returne my Hood.

STR: Take it, least I turne it into some other vse.

CRA: I cant endure the heat of this sun.

STR: I belieue it spoiles y^{r} paint. *aside*

CRA: Ile Maske my face.

STR: Tis so vgly it needes no other Couer.

enter Bra: gadocia.

CRA: Come Strumbo lets goe, vsher me along.

STR: But now I can't goe.

CRA: Whats ye Matter?

STR: I see a Man—An Ague shakes ev'ry ioynt of me.

CRA: A Man? Did'st thou never see a man before?

STR: But this is more then a Man[;] he's a Dane, nay more[;] he's a tamer and destroyer of Giants.

CRA: He's ye Divel I warrant you[;] what are you afraid of?

STR: Would you not haue me feare ye Divell? Without doubt he's to be fear'd[;] wherefore Mother looke to y^{r} selfe[;] Ile leaue you my armes, fight you if y^{r} courage serves, for mine lyes in my heeles[.]

CRA: Wilt thou run away, thou Coward? I thinke thou art none[166] of my son, but some Rustick's. [fol. 57v]

STR: True it is, a Rusticke got me, and I was brought vp amongst Hares.

exit and stands behind ye curtain

CRA: Am I thus left alone? Now I begin to be angry[.]

BRA: Woman be patient, I haue nothing to say to you.

CRA: But I haue something to say to you.

Cra: makes Bra: run out

STR: Courage, Mother[,] Courage: so, so. O braue!

Stro: comes in again

The Monster is fled.

CRA: Now Coward haue at thee.

STR: What doe you meane? Oh! Oh! I must run away[.]

---

[166] Catchword for fols. 57–57v.

CRA: But Ile follow.

ex: Str: Cra:
enter Bra:

BRA: Sure this woman is either Tysiphone or Maegera.[167] Doe ye ffuries all conspire against me? How many misfortunes haue I vndergon? Dwarfs[,] women, my servant, all things are against me. What shall I doe; wch way to take I know not. Pimpo wither art thou run? Why hast thou forsaken thy Master? Wo's me! Now I shall be devoured by thes Rats.

enter Tit: pip:

Sce: 12.

Pipero. Titmus.
Bragadocia.

He see's vs Titmus. We must first fall vpon him.
TIT: Giant defend thyselfe.
PIP: Mighty Statue haue a Care thou fal'st not.
BRA: What now? Whither are these diminutiue animals vanisht? Doe they, peradventure stick vpon my Cloaths?[168] Or haue they hid themselves in my breetches? May be these hungry Lice haue harbour'd themselues in my head, or in my neck or shou[l]ders—what are they[,] no where? Oh! Now they come, Oh! Be mercifull, be mercifull.
PIM: Either prepare y^{r} selfe to fight or yeeld y^{r} selfe a prisoner. [fol. 58]
BRA: Tis A hard Choise. I confesse I could never fight vnlesse with words, and because I never did fight I will not begin now. Wherefore I yeeld myselfe to you, to obey y^{r} pleasures.
PIM: Throw of your Armes.
BRA: Tis don.
TIT: Kneele downe.
BRA: I Kneele.
PIM: Put y^{r} hands to ye ground.
BRA: I doe.
TIT: Now take this Bridle into y^{r} mouth, and put it over y^{r}

---

[167] Tysiphone and Maegera were two of the three Erinnyes, or Furies, who punished crimes and whose horrific heads were wreathed with serpents.

[168] That is, "clothes."

Necke.
BRA: I haue don it.
PIP: Now Titmus get vp. Thou hast overcome thy enimy.
You came hither on foote, but will ride back vpon a horse.
TIT: Or rather vpon an Asse. Thou shalt ride when it comes to thy turne.

exeunt

Sce: 13.

Gormo.

The blustring winds scourge not ye Ocean
with a greater Impetuosity;
nor sweepes ye snow from ye scythian Mountains
with so great a violence, as the Stormes
of Anger agitate the enflamed breast
of Gothurnus, who lyes closly besieg'd[,]
and shut vp into the narrow Confines
of a Castle; where Hunger cruelly
destroys his souldiers which lye dead in heapes [fol. 58v]
before his face; yet his adamantine
Heart relents not; and his obstinate minde
furiously combating with it selfe
regards not these severe Calamities.
As a Rocke beates backe ye soft embraces
of ye waues with a proud repulse; so He
with wrath repells our supplications,
and Complaints though ioyned with threats.
Loe here he comes, disquieted in thoughts.

Sce: 14.

Gothurnus. Osberne. Gormo.

Tis resolu'd. Wee'l all perish togeather.
OSB: Can you thus suffer y^{r} subiects to dye
miserably for hunger, which their loue
to you hath brought from their natiue dwellings?
GOTH: Shall I spare my subiects that would destroy
ye verry Gods; and would anihilate
ye heau'ns; ye earth; all things; and myselfe too
to compleate my Rage.
OSB: A Kingly spirit

ought to be aboue ye reach of Evells.
GOTH: You frame Statuiz'd[169] Kings: A King
ought to resent.
GOR: A King should allwayes haue an absolute
Dominion ore himselfe.
GOTH: A King that looses his Dominions,
looses ye dominion of himselfe.
OSB: What dominion haue you lost?
GOTH: That wch I conquered.
OSB: Was that yours?
GOTH: Tis enough that I conquer'd it. [fol. 59]
OSB: By what Right?
GOTH: By ye Right of war.
OSB: And by the same Right you haue lost it.
GOTH: Lost it? Thats lesse to be endur'd. Lost it?
O ffates! O Gods! O hell! O Heauens!
Do's Gothurnus yet endure it? He can't:
Death is lesse fatall then those words (Lost it.)
Ile therefore dye. But thats a poore revenge.
FFirst let my hand practice on some
audacious enterprize[;] it cant doe lesse:
But dye I will; and rob my Enimy
of that glory; ye hand that lost ye Kingdome,
ye same shall loose ye King. So by my death
I shall triumph over ffate; laugh at my
deceiv'd adversaries, free my subiects
from sorrow, and myselfe from slavery.
Thus you shall see a King dye—Thus, thus Gothurnus—
offers to fall vpon his sword
OSB: Suspend y^{r} rash intent; and he[a]re me speake:
Osb: hinders him
Thinke you to free y^{r} selfe from misery
by a violent death? Be assured,
you will incurre far greater: There's no Crime
more severely feeles ye tartarean[170] fflames
then selfe Murther: Ixion's Wheele[171] inflicts

---

[169] That is "idealized" kings, to be worshipped by fashioning a statue in commemoration.

[170] Adjectival form of the place where Prometheus and other Titans were tortured. A good example of the Christianization of classical myth that was so much a part of Drury's dramatic work.

[171] Ixion was lashed with serpents to a wheel driven endlessly around.

an easy torment; the reiterated labour
of Scisiphus[172] his roleing Stone affords
a pleasure; The thirst of Tantalus[173]
still catching at ye still vncought ffruite,
and often stooping to y^{e} as often deluding
waters; and ye Hart of Titius[174] allwayes
healing to receiue new wonds, are pleasant
punishments compared to ye Tortures
y^{r} Death will bring. O if y^{r} hart retaines [fol. 59v]
any thing of a King; or if any innate
vertue lodges in y^{r} breast, reclaime y^{r} thoughts
from so foule, so horrid a fait,[175] wch was halfe
already don in being so neere doing.
GOR: Great Prince, receiue our supplications
with a condescending Eare. By y^{r} owne
Genius, by whatsoever is deare,
and precious to you I aske by it;
ffor Osbern's sake—
GOTH: Ha! For Osbern's sake; tis hard to deny,
harder to grant: Osberne alas is dead;
and doe I liue? He's gon to th' Infernall
shades, and shall not I follow? Be bold my Hand[;]
finish what even now you wer so neare.
offers again to fall vpon his sword.
OSB: O Hold. Ile teach you a more easy way
of dying, a way which will be also
pervious to æternity:[176] if you
Covet to dye, assault y^{r} enimies;
so, you may obtain either a laurell
of victory or Death: Are you not yet
mou'd? Grant at least this satisfaction
to y^{r} ffriend, that with ye hand you intend
to murther yourselfe, you'l first dispatch me.

---

[172] That is, "Sisyphus," who was doomed forever to roll a great stone up a hill only to have it fall back again before ever reaching the top.

[173] The text decribes in detail the punishment of this Titan, a Senecan favorite, who appears at the beginning of *Thyestes*.

[174] A giant and son of Earth who was punished for assaulting Leto by being stretched out while vultures preyed upon his ever-renewed liver—*O.C.D.*, s.v. "Tityus."

[175] That is, "fate."

[176] As applied to Gothurnus, the phrase means that he will be able to "enter" (the realm of) eternity.

Behold my breast lyes open to y^{r} sword.
GOR: Rather turn it vpon me.
OSB: Doe you deny this too?
GOR: Are you still obstinate?
OSB: You are then an impious selfe murtherer.
GOR: A Tyrant.
OSB: Insolent. [fol. 60]
GOR: Barbarous.
GOTH: Ha. Ha.
OSB: The destruction of y^{r} Cuntry.
GOR: An Invader of anothers.
OSB: Treacherous to y^{r} friends.
GOTH: I laugh at these Reproaches.
OSB: That Osberne whose Exequie[177] you deplore
was an infamous Murtherer.
GOR: Gormo was a villainous Thiefe.
GOTH: Thou ly'st. And Thou.
OSB: Osberne was an incestuous Ravisher.
GOR: They both haue paid condigne punishments
To their Enimy.
OSB: And to Heau'n.
GOTH: And so shall both of you to me. If that
torment wch brings death, can be enough
to satisfy my ffury. If there were a death
beyond death I would inflict it. But this
you ask'd, and you shall haue it; and from my hand.
This deed Ile sacrifize to my Brother
runs at Osb: and gor:
To Gormo, and to myselfe—
they pull of their periwigs
What suddain Horrour seases on my ioynts,
and benums my hand? I tremble with chilnesse
and Amazement on all sides confounds me.
Behold my Brothers Ghost. Behold Gormo's;
They'r come, I know, to reproach my tardy
Resolution of Death; and to chide
my demurring Hand, sloathfull in taking
A iust Revenge from their Adversary.

177 "Funeral rites; funeral ceremony"—*OED*, s.v. "exequy."

And doe I yet delay? Gothurnus ffall— [fol. 60v]
offers again to fall vpon his sword.
Osb: prevents him
OSB: FForbeare. We are not as you imagine
Airy Spirits, and phanticke Gohsts.[178] Those that
you see, you see aliue. An Enimy
Hath snatch'd vs from ye greedy iawes of death,
and gaue vs life and you a ffriend, and Brother.
An Enimy, tis true, made vs suffer
equally to our Crime; and an Enimy
Hath apply'd redresses to our suff'rings.
Our foes are friends you see, and harbour not
perpetuall Hatred, nor doth their ffury
generate a neverending Mallice.
They overcome by Piety: such Armes
obtaine a truely glorious Victory.
Wherefore, Brother, after my Example
embrace y^r^ friend[l]y Enimies, embrace
their ffaith, and embrace their worship
of ye true God, heau'n and earth's Creator.
Besides, generous Alfrede offers you a part
In his Kingdome. Yeelde to God, and ffortune.
GOTH: I yeelde. And loose my hatred; Deare Brother,
in thy embraces; and quite forgetting
all my rage Gormo, I run into thy Armes.
I agnize[179] the Christian ffaith, and yeelde
to God, to Piety, to my Brother.
Let Alfrede strait be cald; Let our Herauld
Invite him securely to his Tryumph.
And doth Osberne liue? Tis enough. I haue
won ye day, enioying him in safety.
No part of my lost Kingdom is wanting.

178 That is, "ghosts."
179 "To recognize"—*OED*, s.v. "Agnize."

Sce: 15. ɧ

[fol. 61]

Gothurnus. Alfrede. Humfrey.
Athelrede. Osberne. Gormo.
Souldiers. Attendants.

Whom no day yet hath ever seene subdu'd,
Gothurnus now confesses himselfe vanqui[s]h't
By y^r Armes, by y^r faith, and Piety[,]
disowning our false and impotent Gods,
to be Alfred's Captiue, and disciple
In ye service of ye true Deity,
And with all mine, become y^r Proselyte.[180]
ALF: Gothurnus, accept my gratefull returns:
I here promise to be a friend to you,
And faithfull to all yours. Nor shall you want
A Kingdome, ffor where great Britane confronts
The rising Sun,[181] you shall rule its Poeple
both numerous, and potent, and shall be
enstaul'd their Soverain: Thus I'm content
To part Dominions. Now let war cease;
And Peace vnlocke its treasures; whilst we sing
Hymnes of Prayses to Heau'ns æternall King.

exeunt

Epilogue

[fol. 61v]

S^t. Cuthbert.

Alfrede exil'd, and from his Princely State
divorc'd did in A Cottage dwell of late,
Now Heau'n doth reinthrone him, and, you see
Invests with great Britaine's Monarchy:
The world can boast, but few that like him are
I[n] learning, ffaith, in Piety in warre.
O wretched England! Would thou still did'st know
that ancient happy state; thou wouldst not now
As from ye world thou seperated art,

---

180 A "proselyte" is a convert.
181 Signifying that the Danes will rule East Anglia.

So from y^e worlds true faith be kept apart:
Thou wouldst not then be cald an Isle ingrate
ffrom Heau'n rebelliously degenerate;
Nor wouldst thou consecrated Temples spoile,
Nor them with sacrilegious Hands defyle;
Nor let vnparent=like thy Children bee
Shipwrackt vpon y^e Rockes of Herisy.
But England's now a Stepmother, alas,
which once of Saints a fertile Parent was.

disapeares

ffinis
Laus Deo.[182]
1659

[182] Praise be to God.

Appendix I

The Epilogue To *Aluredus*

[Knightley translates the first seventeen lines of Drury's epilogue. The untranslated remainder is presented below.[1] Since Knightley refocuses the emphasis of Drury's epilogue, the entire epilogue in the original Latin follows the translation.]

Lo! by bloodshed Alfred won the laurel wreath for you [O England!] from the enemy of the faith, whom you now suffer to triumph anew. Alfred with victorious arm protected the Roman religion, and you betray it to the foe—if indeed that can be called an evil which you had earlier imbibed from a poisonous parent. O devoted band of youth, hope of an island in the midst of shipwreck, you who are like to a spark of the faith cast from a great fire, from which the fatherland will shine with a brighter flame, take up the arms of piety, not those dedicated to terrible Mars such as the giants bear: by taking up the Christian arms, doctrine and faith, conquer by enduring. There is no greater victory than this. By patient sufferance evil is vanquished. Young men, wage such battles. Weary the deity with frequent prayer; the army of heaven will bring every assistance. Your chorus of martyrs will approach triumphant over the menaces of Avernus. Be bold. Deliverance will certainly come in the end.

Epilogus

St. Cuthbertus

Qui paene adempto profugus imperio fuit,
Et latuit humilis incola Alvredus casae;
Deo annuente, Regna maiora occupat;
Monarcha mox futurus et regni caput:
Tulere paucos secula huic regi viros

[1] The basis for this translation is Edgar Hall, who translates lines 18–22 and 24–34 in his introduction to *Aluredus* (23–24). My Latinist colleague, Zoja Pavlovskis reviewed Hall's work and fleshed out the remainder in this conservative translation.

Pietate similes, Marte, doctrina, fide.
O utinam avito non recessisses statu
Anglia; nec, orbe sicut excluso cares,
Ita caruisses orbis exclusi fide!
Ingrata superis insula, rebellis Deo
Non dicereris: nec sacra aequaraes solo
Culmina, paterno gravius oceano tumens,
Dum facta avorum, et pristinos mores fugis.
Tot filiorum naufragia merens pati
Non cogereris, quos procelloso impetu
Erroris unda, atque aestus in Syrtes rapit,
Noverca facta, quae prius fueras parens,
Alvredus ecce sanguine paravit tibi
Ab hoste fidei lauream hunc pateris novos
De te triumphos ferre. Romanam fidem
Victoriosa texit Alvredus manu:
Hanc prodis hosti: si tamen tamen hoc scelus
Poterit vocari, quod venenosa hauseras
Prius a prente. Turba vos iuvenum pia,
Spes naufragantis insulae, et fiedi velut
Scintilla magnis eruta ex incendiis,
Ardebit unde patria meliori face,
Pietatis arma sume; non illa horrido
Devota Marti, qualia gigantes gerunt:
Sed illa Christiana doctrinam, fidem,
Patiendo vince. Maius hoc nullum genus
Victoriae est. FERENDO superanatur mala.
Haec gerite iuvenes praelia; frequenti prece
Numen fatigate. Omnis auxilium feret
Militia caeli: Martyrum vester chorus
Aderit triumphans contra Avernales minas.
Audete. SER o veniet, et CERTO salus.

FINIS

Appendix II

Pedigrees of the Blounts and Knightleys

THE BLOUNTS OF SODINGTON, Devonshire

Sir Walter Blount, Baronet of Sodington, Dev. (b. ca. 1594; m. Elizabeth, dau. of Tichbourne; estates confiscated by Parliament, 1652; d. 1654)

11 children, including:
—Thomas and Edward, who attended the College at Douai;

—John, Peter, Will, who fought for Charles I;

—SIR GEORGE BLOUNT, 2d Baronet (and heir), Worc., m. MARY KIRKHAM
7 children, including Sir Walter Kirkham Blount, 3d. Baronet (heir, m. twice; children d. young; d. 1717 without issue; title passed to nephew)

—ELEANOR (probably youngest daughter) married
1. ROBERT KNIGHTLEY "the Recusant" of Off-Church (m. 1642>-<1652; widowed 1655).* By this marriage Robert became MARY (KIRKHAM) BLOUNT's brother-in-law
2 children,
Thomas (d. young)
Elizabeth

2. Walter Aston, 3d Baron (m. 1655>), whose mother, Mary Weston, was d. of Catholic minister Richard Weston, Earl of Portland
7 children, including
Edward-Walter, first-born, 1658

THE KNIGHTLEYS OF OFF-CHURCH, Warwickshire

Edward Knightley (d. 1614), married
1. Elizabeth Thacker
2. Elizabeth Lenthall (d. 1612)
3. Elizabeth Knolles
Children (mothers are identified by number)
1. Valentine (d. young)
2. Edward (d. young)
2. George (d. young)
2. Edward (b. 1588) studied at St. Omer's and Valladolid, 1600–1609; father of John Marins, Benedictine Monk

Also, 6 daughters, including, Elizabeth, a nun at Lisbon; and Dorothy, a Poor Clare

2. Andrew (d. 1660; Priest, Papal Vicar-General, godfather of ROBERT KNIGHTLEY, translator)
2. ROBERT KNIGHTLEY of Off-Church, "the Recusant" (1576–1655), married
   1. Anne Pettus (or Pettous) (d. 1629)
      Children include Sir John Knightley, Baronet and heir (1610–1650), whose son Sir John Knightley, 2nd Baronet (1630–1688) embraced Anglicanism before his death
   2. Mary (Oldham) Kirkham (widow of Richard Kirkham, 1630; rem. c. 1631–34; d. <1642)

      By Richard Kirkham:

      MARY KIRKHAM (b. 1628; sole daughter and heir, 1630; m. George Blount; dedicatee of *Alfrede* 1659–60, becoming step-daughter of Robert Knightley "the Recusant" after mother's second marriage)

      By ROBERT KNIGHTLEY "the Recusant":

      ROBERT KNIGHTLEY (translator of *Alfrede* 1632>-1684, and half-brother of his dedicatee LADY MARY (KIRKHAM) BLOUNT; had 2 daughters) Valentine Knightley (1633>-alive 1688; d. without issue)
   3. ELEANOR BLOUNT (m. 1642>-<1652; widowed 1655; younger sister of George Blount)
      2 children by this marriage (see under BLOUNT)

* >=after
<=before

Textual Notes

Dedication 6. w^{ch}] without period beneath the ch
7. ex=[/]terne] here and throughout the manuscript, the equal sign followed by an editorially inserted slash [/] signifies a scribal line break in a prose section of the manuscript
8. communicate] second c superimposed on anticipatory t
22. live] l superimposed on original r [?]
The Names of y^{e} Actors [Officer to Gothurnus]] character description missing in MS, but Drury lists Rollo in the "Dramatis Personae" as "Centurio"
Gothurnus.] majuscule superimposed on miniscule
[Pimpo . . . Bragadocia]] skipped in list of dramatis personae but included at this point, following Bragodocia's name, in Drury's text as "Pimpo servus militis gloriousi"
Prologue 29. apeare[;]] apear,
31. clad] c overwritten beside uncancelled initial g
Act 1, Scen 1 1. Act: i . . . scen: i.] In MS the notations for the act and the first scene appears on the *same* line
Act 1, Scene 2 2–3. *Ath:* . . . *Hum:*] Except in these first two instances, MS displays speaker abbreviations in margins
11. Athelrede] Athel$_{\wedge}{}^{r}$ede; middle letters written on smudged background
Act 1, Scena 3 7. run[;]] run,
9. mother[;]] mother,
13. obediênce[;]] obediênce,
38. custody[;]] custody,
50. Poverty] v superimposed on original p
53. cover'd[.]] cover'd.
Act 1, Sce 4 29. Squire] last four letters superimposed on unrecoverable original
41. fame] (fame inserted above penultimate word in line
Act 1, Sce 5 12. loose] interlined above obliterated deletion with caret
24. father[,]] father.
24. Kingdome] King$_{\wedge}{}^{dome}$
26. stupifyed] stup$_{\wedge}{}^{if}$yed
44. restor'd] fourth, fifth, and sixth letters superimposed on original word; looped ascender visible after the t
Act 1, Sce 6 1. strange] ng superimposed on original; looped descender visible beneath the n
10. bright] bringht
11. myselfe] ascender of a rejected letter visible above m
Act 1, Sce 7 5. dogs[,]] dogs.
8. catchword missing
19. perish[,]] perish?
20. too[?]] too.
Act 1, Sce 9 10. Why] miniscule w superimposed on neck of original y with descender still visible
Act 1, Sce 10 19. Tis] originally Jis
41. [a]] emendation for I
Act 1, Sce 11 2. Prey] e superimposed on original a
11. learne] learne.
13. throw] throwgh with cancel line through gh
13. catchword missing due to *s.d.* on lower margin
Act 1, Sce 12 4. rage,] comma merged with faded, Roman majuscule S
10. This h] smudged and superimposed with legible lobe of original e between i and s and a looping ascender still visible before h
23. y^{r} cuntry] rare instance of non-raised or barely raised r constrained by the long

descender of the y from line above
34. y^{r} selves] (y^{r}selves below line with period beneath r
47. gift] gift.
50. pursue[,]] pursue.
Act 1, Sce 13 4. incensse] ince^{n}sse
5. quarrel[,]] quarrel?
6. blood[?]] blood.
12. Awfull] A superimposed on unrecoverable original letter
30. brothers[,]] brothers.
47. wth] with period beneath th
64. wickednesse[,]] wickednesse.
Act 1, Sce 14 30. inocence[?]] inocence.
33. Why] W superimposed on unrecoverable letter
39–42. verses bracketed in left-hand margin
51. fledd] fl^{e}dd The word is crowded in by end-of-line *s.d.*, which was penned before the verse line
59. y^{r}] superimposed on the washed out words, by a
63. catchword missing
Act 1, Sce 15 6. wound] wo^{u}nd
18. vndergoe[,]] vndergoe.
33. vs] blotted around s
Act 2, Sce 1 6. armes] vestiges of anticipatory of precede armes The MS has been perforated along the ascender of original f suggesting a second method of erasure—use, perhaps, of a knife point
9. shower] initial minum of w blotted at base
10. its owne] its(owne
15. withall[,]] withall.
30. vaild] a blotted. The initial blotted vowel could possibly have been intended as an e
35. leaues[,]] leaues.
37. Leopard[,]] Leopard.
45. Prize[,]] Prize.
46. wound] wou^{n}d
61. vally[,]] vally.
63. Lambe] first three letters written over a smudged background
75. of] the word appears twice in MS—end l.74, beg. l.75.
80. wth] period beneath th
86. opening] op$_{\wedge}{}^{e}$ning
92. wolues[,]] wolues:
Act 2. Sce 2 1. he] $_{\wedge}{}^{he}$
7. *faints*] ai smudged
15. safety] blurred vertical mark after word might be interpreted as a colon mark
16. an'd] *sic*
20. stands] stan^{d}s
Act 2. Sce 3 2. Idoll] Idoll.
4. proteous] prote$_{\wedge}{}^{o}$us
5. his] his,
Act 2. Sce 4 24. with] appears twice consecutively
33. who] w superimposed on original letter with ascender
37. all] all. [?] A point mark is evident but appears supralinearly
41. briefely[,]] briefely.
45. and] a$_{\wedge}{}^{nd}$
56. Purple] ur superimposed on original r where u now stands; letter subsequent is not discernible
56. wth] with period beneath th
57. my head] $_{\wedge}{}^{my}$
60. sunne] u superimposed on original o
61. Now] boldly superimposed on washed out original, with vestigial eye of l visible between N and o
Act 2. Sce 5 1. scilla] over the i two vertical period marks appear, the higher one faded,

the lower not
32. Companions[;]] Companions,
32. Poverty] v superimposed on original p
32. thee] following this word, the word poore is deleted
Act 2. Sce 6 1–2. attempted obliteration of bracketed (but not underlined) *s.d.* continues in margin to catchword. The discernible cancelled words appear to be, "Stru gets into / ye body of . . . / of ye tree and / peeps out of / ye top"
2. I[,]] I?
6. to] superimposed t with double cross-bar legible
8. I] in MS, I'le The auxiliary verb is supererogatory. Sentence makes sense either by reading "I'le venture" or "I must venture"
13. *gets . . . tree*] cancelled *s.d.* is partially restored here at the end of the prose passage
28. catchword missing
56. catchword missing
57. *peeps . . . tree*] remainder of cancelled *s.d.* is restored here in accordance with events signified in the text
58. too[?]] too.
60. tis y^{rs} . . . y^{rs}] both ^{rs} supralineations show period beneath
72. is] 'twixt deleted after the word
74. or] o superimposed on original letter, ascender of which is visible
75. is] is:
76. Aile[;]] Aile,
Act 2. Sce 7 4. catchword missing
6. itch't[;]] itch'd,
7. with] stray oblique graph from left of w to line below
20. bastard] r superimposed on obscured original letter
21. out[,]] out.
24. a] a.
26. rogue] rogue.
27. charge] cha^{r}ge
31. *Str:*] *r* superimposed on original *t*
34. nam'd] interlined above deleted word, made
48–57. *he coughs . . . again*] Directions in this sequence are not underlined, but the episode is one of the few for which Drury provides directions
55. deserv'd[,]] deserv'd.
60. catchword missing
Act 2. Sce 8 2. keepes[,]] keepes?
3. so] $_{\wedge}^{so}$
14. iourney[,]] iourney.
24. me] me?
26. stealer[?] stealer.
39. f[ro]m] emendation for form
43. out] original word, of, anticipating subsequent word, is overwritten
47. mee] mee.
49. all[;]] all,
61. victorious] initial minum of u partially covers original a [?]
78. Edifices] first five letters superimposed on smudged original
Act 3. Sce 1 1. Act: 3 . . . Sce: i #] In MS the notation for the act and first scene appears on the *same* line
10. catchword missing
16. perfidious] first three letters superimposed on original; beneath the stem of the r a vestigial descender is visible
38. catchword missing
39. her[,]] her?
39. yet] superimposed and not altogether legible
39. will[?]] will.
Act 3. Scen 3 6. liue[;]] liue,
Act 3. Sce 4 6. breath] breath.
7. poysoned] although lined through in MS, the word is essential to the sentence

9. well[;]] well,
16. Counsellors] Cou^{n}sellors
67. heare] ar superimposed on original word
Act 3. Sce 5 5. with] the word clouds deleted after with
59. feete] t evidently superimposed on original l
Act 3. Sce 6 49. catchword missing
52. r[u]n] ran
59. with[;]] with,
79. speake] final s cancelled
99. me[.]] me,
120. tree] tree;
Act 3. Sce 7 2. blows] blows?
3. hither[?]] hither:
9. pronounc'd] ascender appears over the back of c anticipating d
11. vnexperienced] vnexperien'ced The apostrophe is probably vestigial since c and e are superimposed on what appears to have been a 'd whose looped ascender is still visible above final e
17. yealld] yeal^{l}d
29. wherein] wh superimposed on a letter whose ascender is visible along with a second letter bearing a descender
31. eradicate] r superimposed on original d [?]
34. catchword missing
37. me] ‸^{me}
45. am[,]] am.
Act 3. Sce 9 2. Cell[,]] Cell:
13. salvage] v superimposed on original g
30. stir[,]] stir.
48. you[;] you,
49. wounds] superimposed on blurred original with vestigial ascender visible above w and descender below n
56. of] ‸^{of}
65. armes[;]] armes,
Act 3. Sce 10 9. shamefully] s^{h}amefully
Act 3. Sce 11 11. wounds[,]] wounds.
17. nere] ‸^{n}ere
19. throne]] throne?
35. earth] e superimposed on initial letter a
Act 3. Sce 12 2. was[,]] was.
Act 3. Sce 15 10. beneficiall] ben^{e}ficiall
40. Brother[,]] Brother.
46. them[,]] them.
69. a King] emendation for I King
Act 4. Sce 1 5. sanctity] sanctity.
7. beeing] bee superimposed on original. The remains of an se appear before the b with attempted erasure of s using knife point [?]—the paper is abraded
13. endure] The scribe has attempted to correct the letter after d. The original letter e is clearly legible
Act 4. Sce 2 4. Winde[,]] Winde?
6. saild] l superimposed on original d
51. cloath'd[,]] cloath'd.
60. I] ‸^{I}
72. Minde] Minde!
73. God[!]] God.
75. had bin] circular blot .3 centimeters in diameter between words
87. Assistance] smudged A superimposed on original s [?]
93. y^{r}] smudged around the y which is superimposed on original o [?]
97. acknowledge] c superimposed on original k with shank still visible
113. give] lobe of g blotted; cross stroke of original letter visible
131. possesse.] possesse..

Act 4. Sce 3 7. wth] period beneath th
Act 4. Sce 4 7. you[.]] you,
21. Gods] vowel has downstroke characteristic of an a
Act 4. Sce 5 Denve[v]ulphe] Denephulphe Another example of scribal anticipation—here of the final syllable
9. suggests] initial g originally b or l
Act 4. Sce 6 S$^{t.}$] beneath the word an interlinear blot .5 centimeters in diameter
19. selfe.] selfe..
25. encreast[;]] encreast,
29–30. fishponds.] On right margin beneath fishponds is an obliterated *s.d.* of two lines. See discussion in Introduction on the scribal character of this and other cancelled directions under "The Manuscript"
Act 4. Sce 7 Denevulphe] v superimposed on original p
16. wth] period beneath th
18. turn'd] u superimposed on unrecoverable original letter
28. ourseleues] oursel‸^{e}ues
Act 4. Sce 8 15. you] ^{you}
21. had] ‸^{had}
25. I] ^{I}
30. a[nd]] emendation for at
35. I] ‸^{I}
Act 4. Sce 10 15. Conquest[—]] Conquest.
15. returne] t badly smeared
18. to] ^{to}
34. [r]e[l]iefe] emendation for lesiefe
Act 4. Sce 11 10. signes] n superimposed on original h [?]
11. return'd,] return'd,:
Act 4. Sce 12 7. them] ‸^{them}
10. so] ^{so}
Act 4. Sce 13 12. dye] d superimposed on original l
12. their] t superimposed on original y
26. friend[;]] friend,
Act 4. Sce 14 13. vnassaulted[,]] vnassaulted?
15. Misfortunes[?]] Misfortunes.
18. teares] tea superimposed on faded, blotted g or y
22. Athelnea[,]] Athelnea:
28. rest[;]] rest,
48. expect] e superimposed on original a or o
Act 4. Sce 15 7. togeather] tog smudged and superimposed on original, with d still visible
10. to] original ascender visible above o
20. [Athelnea.]] editor's interpolation for missing place name
21. shrowding] r interposed after stem word was written
Act 4. Sce 16 15. Menaces[;]] Menaces,
26. lucidly] ci superimposed on prematurely written d
30. storme[,] storme;
31. Cell[;]] Cell,
Act 4. Sce 17 6. you[,]] you.
8. Englands] initial n superimposed on a letter with visible ascending loop
13. grieue] g^{r}ieue
21. law[;]] law,
50. Mother[;]] Mother,
67. which[.]] which,
68. both[;]] both,
69. happy[;]] happy,
77. Pious] scribal correction of original Piety
87. are] repeated and cancelled in MS
88. vertue] v bears similitude to original w
91. w^{t}] with period beneath ^{t}

93. ought] ou‸^{gh}t
107. Courage] Cour^{a}ge
117. *Enter. Osb: Gor:*] Whereas *Aluredus* commences a new scene (18) at this point, the scene continues in *Alfrede*
118. dye] ie: inserted above ye but not deleted; supralinear letter before ie: obscured
135. enioyes[;]] enioyes.
Act 4. Sce 1[8] 1[8]] 19 in MS Having conflated scenes 17 and 18 of Drury's edition, Knightley neglects to renumber this next scene and simply continues the scene count as Drury has it. For the hypothesis that this inadvertence may suggest Knightley's use of the 1641 edition of Drury's works, see Introduction under, "The Translation"
8. to th'] anticipatory h still evident over o
20. scarce] supererogatory (before scarce Following scarce but cancelled with a single line is the word, fixt
38. heare] he^{a}re
62. ioy[;]] joy,
Act 5. Sce 2 4. horses[,]] horses.
10. w^{ch}] without period beneath ^{ch}
16. thousand] tho^{u}sand
27. nothing[,]] nothing.
28. herring[?]] herring.
33. *Pip:*] emendation for *Tit* but Pipero is the intended speaker since Titmus speaks before and after
34. Polemobombardifragosogiganiomachopumponides] with period after the word
35. Althô] inserted from bottom-right corner of margin after the word Revenge. (# notation signifies place of insertion.) Catchword consequently missing due to insertion of ‸^{Althô} in place where catchword would originally be placed
Act 5. Sce 3 5. wth] period beneath th
14. me] me,
Act 5. Sce 4 10. *Alf*] MS has *Bra* twice consecutively. Drury designates Alfrede as the speaker here
Act 5. Sce 5 1. complain[,]] complain?
10. Anger] smeared descender of g superimposed with signs of abrasion evident
12. brother[;]] brother,
19. reeling] r superimposed on l [?]
68. nimblenesse] ni‸^{m}blenesse
87. Thirst[;]] Thirst,
97. late[;]] late,
Act 5. Sce 6 8. into] word written on a smudged background
8. spoile[,]] spoile.
15. deluded[,]] deluded?
17. su[b]du'd] emendation for uncorrected anticipatory d in suddu'd Cf. 5.14.1 where Gothurnus again expresses the feeling of being subdued
22. doe I] doe ^{I}
23. infernall] r superimposed on original l
34. souldiers] souldiers.
51. lawrell[;]] lawrell,
Act 5. Sce 8 5. [crown?]] A word is missing. The line following suggests it is probably Gothurnus's crown
Act 5. Sce 9 5. he] interlined above deletion, you
9. money[;]] money,
Act 5. Sce 10 25. mad[;]] mad,
25. Im] The second letter is unclear and appears to have been a correction for an errant ve
26. yeares] head of y superimposed on unrecoverable original letter
26. younger] yo‸^{u}nger
26. agoe[;]] agoe,
36. rare[,]] rare?
38. face[?]] face.
Act 5. Sce 11 2. Take[—]] Take,

16. Man[;]] Man,
18. Divel] l superimposed on obscured original letter
18. you[;]] you,
20. fear'd[;]] fear'd,
21. selfe[;]] selfe,
25. a Rusticke] a and R written over a smudged background
Act 5. Sce 12 26. ride] interlined above the deletion, goe, with caret
Act 5. Sce 13 6. besieg'd[,]] besieg'd.
8. Hunger] original a overwritten by e
Act 5. Sce 14 2. you] ^{you}
30. enterprize[;]] enterprize,
55. was] last two letters superimposed on original letters, with a right-looping descender still visible
65. Hand[;]] Leeching may be responsible for the mark after the word that looks like a comma
67. Ile] I^{le}
67. easy] e superimposed on original a
91. a] ^{a}
98. torment] interlined above deleted word, sacrifice
Act 5. Sce 15 3. Piety[,]] Piety.
11. great] ‸^{great}

Bibliography

Primary Sources

Drury, William. *Aluredus sive Alfredus Tragicomoedia ter exhibita, in seminario anglorum duaceno ab eiusdem collegii iuventute, anno Domini MDCXIX*. Douai: Ioannis Bogardus, 1620.

———. *Dramatica Poemata. Editio secunda ab ipso authore recognita, & multo quam prima auctior reddita*. Douai: Ioannis Bogardus, 1628.

———. *Dramatica Poemata. Editio ultima ab ipso auctore recognite, & multo quam prima auctior reddita*. Antwerp and Douai: P. Bellerus, 1641.

R. K. *Alfrede or Right Reinthron'd*. [1659–60]. MS. Rawlinson. poet. 80. Bodleian Library, Oxford Univ.

Secondary Sources

Acts of the Privy Council, 1617–1619. 32 vols. N.S. Ed. John R. Dasent. London, 1890.

Akrigg, G. P. V. *Jacobean Pagant or the Court of James I*. 1962. Repr. New York: Athenaeum, 1974.

Anstruther, Godfrey. *The Seminary Priests, A Dictionary of the Secular Clergy of England and Wales 1558–1850*. Vol. 2. Great Wakering, Essex: Mayhew-McCrimmon, 1975.

Asser, Bishop of Sherborne. *Alfred the Great: Asser's Life of King Alfred and other Contemporary Sources*. Trans. Simon Keynes and Michael Lapidge. Harmondsworth: Penguin, 1983.

Bald, Robert C. *Donne and the Drurys*. Cambridge: Cambridge Univ. Press, 1959.

Barthes, Roland. "From Work to Text." In *Textual Strategies: Perspectives in Post-Structuralist Criticism*, ed. Josué Harari, 73–81. Ithaca: Cornell Univ. Press, 1979.

Bellenger, Dominic A., ed. *English and Welsh Priests 1558–1800*. Bath, England: Downside Abbey, 1984.

Bentley, G. E. *The Jacobean and Caroline Stage*. 7 vols. Oxford: Clarendon Press, 1941–68.

Binns, J. W. "Seneca and Neo-Latin Tragedy in England." In *Seneca*, ed. C. D. N. Costa, 205–34. London and Boston: Routledge & Kegan Paul, 1974.

Blount, Sir Walter Kirkham, trans. *The Office of the Holy Week According to the Missal and Roman Breviary*. London, 1670.

———. *The Spirit of Christianity*. London, 1686.

Boas, Frederick Samuel. *University Drama in the Tudor Age*. Oxford: Oxford Univ. Press, 1914.

Bossy, John. *The English Catholic Community 1570–1850*. London: Darton, Longman & Todd, 1975.

Bowers, Fredson. *Principles of Bibliographical Description*. Princeton: Princeton Univ. Press, 1949.

Boysse, Ernest. *Le Théâtre des Jesuites*. 1880. Repr. Geneva: Slatkine Reprints, 1970.

Bryant, J. A. "The Significance of Jonson's First Requirement for Tragedy: 'Truth of Argument.'" *Studies in Philology* 49 (1952): 195–213.

Burke's Peerage and Baronetage. 105th ed. Repr. London: Burke's Peerage (Genealogical Books), 1970.

Calendar of the Clarendon State Papers. 5 vols. Ed. F. J. Routledge. Oxford: Clarendon Press, 1932. Vol. 4.

Calendar of State Papers, Domestic Series, Charles I. 23 vols. Ed. John Bruce. 1864. Repr. Nendeln, Lichtenstein: Kraus Reprints, 1967. Vol. 7.

Camden, William. *Anglica, Normannica, Hibernica, Cambrica, a veteribus scripta ex quibus Asser Meneuensis*. Frankfurt, 1602; 2d ed., 1603.

Caraman, Philip. *Henry Garnet, 1555–1606 and the Gunpowder Plot*. London: Longmans, 1964.

Chambers, E. K. *The Elizabethan Stage*. 4 vols. Oxford: Clarendon Press, 1923. Vol. 4.

Charlton, H. B. *The Senecan Tradition in Renaissance Tragedy*. Manchester: Univ. of Manchester Press, 1946.

Churchill, W. A. *Watermarks in Paper in England, France, etc. in the XVIIIII and XVIII Centuries and their Interconnections*. Amsterdam: Menns Hertzberge & Co., 1935.

The Compact Edition of the Oxford English Dictionary: Complete Text Reproduced Micrographically. 2 vols. Oxford: Oxford Univ. Press, 1971.

Croke, Alexander. *The Genealogical History of the Croke Family, Originally Named Le Blount*. 2 vols. Oxford, 1823.

Cunliffe, John W. *The Influence of Seneca on Elizabethan Tragedy*. London: Macmillan, 1893. Repr. New York G. E. Stechert, 1907.

Davies, Godfrey. *The Restoration of Charles II*. San Marino, Calif.: Huntington Library, 1955.

The Dictionary of National Biography. 22 vols. Oxford: Oxford Univ. Press, 1906.

Douay College Diaries, Third, Fourth and Fifth, 1598–1654. Ed. Edwin H. Burton and Thomas L. Williams. London: Catholic Record Society, 1911.

Douce, Francis. *Holbein's Dance of Death*. London: George Bell & Sons, 1884.

Douglas, Robert. *The Peerage of Scotland*. Vol. 1. Edinburgh, 1813.

Dures, Alan. *English Catholicism 1558–1642: Continuity and Change*. Essex, England: Longman, 1983.

The English College at Valladolid: Registers, 1589–1862. Ed. E. Henson. Catholic Record Society. Vol. 30. London: John Whitehead & Son, 1930.

Foley, Henry. *Records of the English Province of the Society of Jesus*. 7 vols. London, 1875–83. Repr. New York: Johnson Repr. Corporation, 1966.

Freeman, Arthur. "William Drury, Dramatist." *Recusant History*. Ed. A. F. Allison and D. M. Rogers. Catholic Record Society 8 (1966): 293–97.

Gillow, Joseph. *A Literary and Biographical History or Bibliographical Dictionary of the English Catholics from the Breach with Rome to the Present Time*. 5 vols. London, 1885–1902. Vol. 2.

Greg, W. W. *English Literary Autographs, 1550–1650*. 2 vols. Oxford: Oxford Univ. Press, 1932. Repr. Nendeln, Lichtenstein: Kraus Reprints, 1968.

Gurr, Andrew. *The Shakespeare Stage, 1574–1642*. Rev. 2d ed. Cambridge: Cambridge Univ. Press, 1980.

Hall, Edgar. "William Drury's *Alvredus sive Alfredus*." Ph.D. diss., Univ. of Chicago, 1918.

Harbage, Alfred. *Annals of English Drama, 975–1700*. Rev. S. Schoenbaum. 1964. Rev. 3d ed. Sylvia S Wagonheim. London and New York: Routledge, 1989.

———. *Cavalier Drama*. New York: Modern Language Association, 1936. Repr. New York: Russell & Russell, 1964.

Holinshed, Raphael. *The Historie of England from the time it was first inhabited vntil the time it was last conquered*. London, 1587.

Holt, Geoffrey. *St. Omers and Bruges Colleges, 1593–1773, A Biographical Dictionary*. London: Catholic Record Society, 1975.

Home, John. *Alfred, a Tragedy*. London, 1778. In *The Plays of John Home*, ed. James S. Malek. New York and London: Garland, 1980.

Hoskins, W. G. *A New Survey of England: Devon*. Newton Abbot: David & Charles, 1972.

Hunter, G. K. "Seneca and the Elizabethans: A Case Study in 'Influence.'" *Shakespeare Survey* 20 (1967): 17–26.

———. "Seneca and English Tragedy." In *Seneca*, ed. C. D. N. Costa, 166–204. London and Boston: Routledge & Kegan Paul, 1974.

Jacquot, Jean, ed. *Les Tragèdies de Senèque et le Théâtre de la Renaissance*. Paris: Centre national de la recherche scientifique, 1964.

Jones, J. R. *Country and Court: England, 1658–1714*. London: Edward Arnold, 1978.

Jonson, Ben. *The Complete Works of Ben Jonson*. Ed. C. H. Herford, and Percy and Evelyn Simpson. 11 vols. Oxford: Clarendon Press, 1925–52.

Kenyon, J. P., ed. *The Stuart Constitution, 1603–1688: Documents and*

Commentary. Cambridge: Cambridge Univ. Press, 1966.

Keynes, Simon, and Michael Lapidge, trans. *Alfred the Great: Asser's Life of King Alfred and Other Contemporary Sources*. Harmondsworth: Penguin, 1983.

Kline, Mary-Jo. *A Guide to Documentary Editing*. Baltimore and London: Johns Hopkins Univ. Press, 1987.

Laslett, Peter. *The World We Have Lost*. 3d Edition. New York: Charles Scribner's Sons, 1984.

Lindley, Keith. "The Part Played by the Catholics." In *Politics, Religion and the English Civil War*, ed. Brian Manning, 127–78. London: Edward Arnold, 1973.

Lucas, F. L. *Seneca and Elizabethan Tragedy*. Cambridge: Cambridge Univ. Press, 1922.

Mendall, Clarence. *Our Seneca*. New Haven: Yale Univ. Press, 1941.

Miller, John. *Popery and Politics in England, 1660–1688*. Cambridge: Cambridge Univ. Press, 1973.

Montrose, Louis. "Professing the Renaissance: The Poetics and Politics of Culture." In *The New Historicism*, ed. H. Aram Veeser, 15–36. New York and London: Routledge, 1989.

Motto, A. L., and John R. Clark. "Senecan Tragedy: A Critique of Scholarly Trends." *Renaissance Drama* 6 (1973): 219–35.

Munday, Anthony, and Henry Chettle, Thomas Dekker, Thomas Heywood, and William Shakespeare. *The Book of Sir Thomas More*. Ed. Vittorio Gabrieli and Giorgio Melchiori. Bari: Adriatica Editrice, 1981.

Nash, Treadway Russell. *Collections for the History of Worcestershire*. 3 vols. London, 1781–82.

Norman, Edward. *Roman Catholicism in England from the Elizabethan Settlement to the Second Vatican Council*. Oxford & New York: Oxford Univ. Press, 1985.

Oliver, George, and J. P. Jones. *Ecclesiastical Antiquities of Devon, Being Observations of Many Churches in Devonshire*. 3 vols. Exeter, 1840–42.

The Oxford Latin Dictionary. Oxford: Clarendon Press, 1968.

Parker, Matthew. *Alfredi Regis res gestae*. London, 1574.

Patterson, Annabel. *Censorship and Interpretation: The Conditions of Writing and Reading in Early Modern England*. Madison: Univ. of Wisconsin Press, 1984.

Petti, Anthony G. *English Literary Hands from Chaucer to Dryden*. Cambridge: Harvard Univ. Press, 1977.

Polwhele, Richard. *The History of Devonshire*. 3 vols. 1793–1806. Repr. Dorking: Kohler & Coombes, 1977.

Potter, Lois. *Secret Rites and Secret Writing: Royalist Literature, 1641–1660*. Cambridge: Cambridge Univ. Press, 1989.

Prince, John. *Danmonii Orientales Illustres: or, The Worthies of Devon.*

1697. Repr. London, 1810.

Public Record Office. Inquisitions Post Mortem. Chancery Series 2. Vol. 464, no. 23.

———. *Inquisitions Post Mortem.* Chancery Series 2. Vol. 521, no. 120.

The Responsa Scholarum of the English College, Rome. Part 1, 1598–1621. Ed. Anthony Kenny. London: Catholic Record Society (Vol. 54.), 1962.

Ross, G. M. "Seneca's Philosophical Influence." In Seneca, ed. C. D. N. Costa, 116–65. London and Boston: Routledge & Kegan Paul, 1974.

Savile, Henry. *Rerum Anglicarum scriptores post Bedam praecipui ... Willielmi Malmesburiensis.* London, 1596. Repr. Aubrij, 1601.

Siconolfi, Michael. "Robert Squire's *Death, A Comedie.*" Ph.D. diss. Syracuse Univ., 1982. Ann Arbor: UMI 8301656.

Sidney, Philip. *An Apology for Poetry.* 1595. Repr. Ed. Forrest G. Robinson. Indianapolis: Bobbs-Merrill, 1970.

Simeon of Durham. *Historiae Anglicanae scriptores x. Simeon Monachus Dunelmensis.* Ed. Roger Twysden. London, 1652.

———. *Symeonis Monachi Opera omnia.* Ed. Thomas Arnold. 2 vols. London, 1857. Repr. London: Kraus, 1965.

Smith, George Charles Moore. *College Plays Performed in the University of Cambridge.* Cambridge: Cambridge Univ. Press, 1923.

A Summary Catalogue of Western Manuscripts in the Bodleian Library at Oxford. Ed. Falconer Madan. Vol. 3. Oxford: Clarendon Press, 1953.

Swanzy, K. T. *The Offchurch Story.* Abingdon, Berkshire: Abbey Press, 1968.

Tannenbaum, Samuel A. *The Handwriting of the Renaissance.* Columbia Univ. Press, 1930. Repr. New York: Frederick Ungar, 1967.

The Tragedy of Locrine. [Anon.] In *Disputed Plays of William Shakespeare,* ed. William Kozlenko. New York: Hawthorn Books, 1974.

The Trial of Treasure. [Anon.] *Early Engish Dramatists: Anonymous Plays.* 3rd. series. Ed. John S. Farmer. 1906. Repr. New York: Barnes and Noble, 1966.

Tricomi, Albert. "Philip Earl of Pembroke and the Analogical Way of Reading Political Tragedy." *Journal of English and Germanic Philology* 85 (1986): 332–45.

Underdown, David. *Royalist Conspiracy in England 1649–1660.* New Haven: Yale Univ. Press, 1960.

Victoria History of the Counties of England: Warwickshire. 8 Vols. 1904–69. London: Oxford Univ. Press for the Univ. of London Institute of Historical Research. Repr. London: Dawsons of Pall Mall, 1965–69.

Victoria History of the Counties of England: Worcestershire. 4 Vols. 1901–24. Repr. Folkestone & London: for the Univ. of London Institute of Historical Research by Dawsons of Pall Mall, 1971.

Visitations of the County of Devon Comprising the Heralds' Visitations of

1531, 1564, and 1620. Ed. John L. Vivian. Exeter, 1895.

The Visitation of the County of Warwick in the Year 1619. Taken by William Camden. Ed. John Fetherston. London, 1877.

Wells, H. W. "Senecan Influence on Elizabethan Tragedy: A Re-Estimation." *Shakespeare Association Bulletin* 19 (1944): 71–84.

William of Malmesbury. *Willelmi Malmesbiriensis monachi gesta regum Anglorum, atque historia novella*. Ed. Thomas D. Hardy. 2 vols. London: English Historical Society, 1840. Repr. Vaduz: Kraus Reprints, 1964.